MARGARET

The Great English Walk

Volume Two: Hathersage to Berwick-upon-Tweed

Margaret and Brian Nightingale

The Great English Walk
Volume 2 (Hathersage to Berwick-upon-Tweed)
1st Edition

Published by
Nightingale Publications
23 Grange Road, BIDDULPH, Staffordshire Moorlands ST8 7SB

Printed and Typeset in Great Britain by
Vibrant Graphics Limited
Radnor Works, 5 Back Lane, CONGLETON, Cheshire CW12 4PP

A British catalogue record for this book is available from the British Library.

ISBN for complete set of 2 volumes: 0 9529490 0 8
ISBN for this volume: 0 9529490 2 4

ISBN for Volume One: 0 9529490 1 6

Front cover: Margaret crossing Hebden Water
Back cover: Plankey Bridge

Copies of this book and Volume 1 may be obtained from
Nightingale Publications, 23 Grange Road, BIDDULPH, Staffordshire Moorlands ST8 7SB.

The book is dedicated to all our friends
who have offered us encouragement.

The Country Code

■ Enjoy the countryside and respect its life and work

■ Guard against all risk of fire

■ Fasten all gates

■ Keep dogs on leads and under close control at all times

■ Keep to public paths across farmland

■ Use gates and stiles to cross farmland

■ Leave livestock, crops and machinery alone

■ Take your litter home, or carry to the nearest disposal point

■ Help to keep all water clean

■ Protect wildlife, plants and trees

■ Take special care when walking on, or crossing roads

■ Make no unnecessary noise

Contents

Page

Introduction   7

Note: The following sections are only a suggestion. Please do sort out for yourselves what mileage suits you, and do less (or more) according to your capabilities. A facility list at the end of the book gives ideas of where you could break the mileage differently.

Section		Miles	km	Page
21	Hathersage to Flouch	20.25	32.4	12
22	Flouch to Holmfirth	8.75	14.0	24
23	Holmfirth to Ripponden	15.0	24.0	30
24	Ripponden to Hebden Bridge	8.0	12.8	38
25	Hebden Bridge to Haworth	11.0	17.6	43
26	Haworth to Ilkley	16.5	26.4	51
27	Ilkley to Pateley Bridge	18.5	29.6	64
28	Pateley Bridge to Masham	17.8	28.5	72
29	Masham to Leyburn	16.4	26.2	79
30	Leyburn to Marrick	11.3	18.1	85
31	Marrick to Barnard Castle	22.0	35.2	90
32	Barnard Castle to Eggleston	6.7	10.7	100
33	Eggleston to Stanhope	16.8	26.9	104
34	Stanhope to Blanchland	13.4	21.4	113
35	Blanchland to Allendale Town	11.0	17.6	120
36	Allendale Town to Bardon Mill	9.6	15.4	124
37	Bardon Mill to Wark	13.6	21.8	130
38	Wark to Elsdon	17.4	27.8	138
39	Elsdon to Rothbury	14.0	22.4	147
40	Rothbury to Uswayford	19.5	31.2	155
41	Uswayford to Wooler	17.9	28.6	162
42	Wooler to Ford	11.9	19.0	167
43	Ford to Norham	13.2	21.1	174
44	Norham to Berwick-upon-Tweed	9.5	15.2	180
App	Optional extra to Scottish Border	5	8.0	186

Facility List   190

GEW Route Map

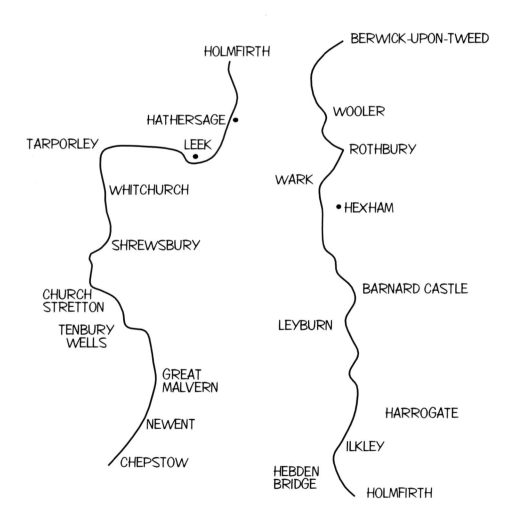

Introduction

WHY?

Having walked most of the long distance paths in the north of Britain, it has long been a dream to establish an alternative south to north, and west to east, path in the UK. The 3 main existing south-to-north routes- the Pennine Way, Offa's Dyke, and the West Highland Way- together with the 2 west to east routes- the Coast to Coast and the Southern Upland Way -are all deservedly very popular, but this route offers something different. A route from Chepstow at the southeast end of Wales, to Berwick-upon-Tweed, almost at the southeast end of Scotland, offers both a south-to- north route and at the same time a west- to- east route. The route is not a straight line between the 2 ends, but is designed to bypass the Midland conurbations, then swing east round the north of Stoke, in order to continue north again.

There are some 140,000 miles of public rights of way in England and Wales. This walk uses some 600-odd miles of these footpaths to explore some of the best scenery that England has to offer. The really dedicated walker could add on the Southwest Peninsula and Severn Ways to get from Land's End, and then devise a route from the border just north of Berwick all the way to John o' Groats!

The only name for the walk had to be The *Great English Walk* (or GEW). We hope that, in time, the walk will become recognised as an official long distance walk and signposted throughout. The only appropriate sign seems to be that great English emblem – the *OAK LEAF*.

PERSONAL

The description of the walk is as we found it in 1996/7, and to some extent is a personal record of our journey. The text has been written in the third person for ease of reading. Most of the route was walked in one go, with stops at Bed and Breakfast establishments. The start of the second volume was a case of driving car to a section's north end, leave a bike with a friendly shopkeeper or inn, drive to the southern end of the section and leave the car, walk the section, pick up the bike, Brian then cycled back on a road to the car, and then drove back to the north end to pick up Margaret.

MAPS GENERAL

The only maps produced by the Ordnance Survey showing paths in detail (and easy to obtain) are the Pathfinder 1:25,000. It is expensive to equip yourself with a full set

The Oak Leaf – The GEW Symbol

of required Pathfinders, but fortunately the OS now produce a series of Leisure 1:25,000 maps which cover the ground of quite a few Pathfinder maps. A new range of Explorer 1:25,000 maps is also now becoming available, and it is hoped that , in time, these will cover all the route.

MAPS IN BOOK

All maps in this book are 1:25,000 (or 2.5 inches to one mile). North is always to the top of the page maps. The maps are based upon Ordnance Survey 1:25,000 mapping with the permission of The Controller of HMSO ©Crown Copyright 85793M 08/97.

SYMBOLS USED

Many guide books are written showing whether the walk follows a hedge, fence or stone wall, but in our experience these usually clutter the map – and do change! Therefore hedges, stiles, steps, gates etc are not usually shown. There was a television programme many years ago where a farmer with land on the Pennine way was interviewed. He said *'I'm fed up with all these walkers...Wainwright said go through the gate painted white...I've foxed 'em, I've painted it red!'* That is why these maps have been kept relatively simple.

ACCOMMODATION

Walkers preferences vary, from hotels to guest houses to camping. We have found that the best way to obtain accommodation is to use the Ramblers Association yearbook list of B & B's, supplemented with contacting Tourist Information Centres along the route.

TOURIST INFORMATION OFFICES

The following is a list of offices on, or near, the route together with telephone numbers—

Alnwick	(01665) 510665
Ashbourne	(01335) 343666
Bakewell	(01629) 813227
Barnard Castle	(01833) 690909
Berwick-upon-Tweed	(01289) 330733
Chepstow	(01291) 623772
Chester	(01244) 317962
Church Stretton	(01694) 723133
Congleton	(01260) 298243
Halifax	(01422) 368725
Haworth	(01535) 642329
Hebden Bridge	(01422) 843831
Hexham	(01434) 605225
Holmfirth	(01484) 687603
Ilkley	(01943) 602319
Ledbury	(01531) 636147
Leek	(01538) 381000
Leyburn	(01969) 623069
Malvern	(01684) 892289
Much Wenlock	(01952) 727679
Newent	(01531) 822145
Pateley Bridge	(01423) 711147
Rothbury	(01669) 620887
Shrewsbury	(01743) 350761
Skipton	(01756) 792809
Stanhope	(01388) 527650
Tenbury Wells	
summer only	(01584) 810136
if closed ring	(01568) 616460
Whitchurch	(01948) 664577
Wooler	(01668) 281602

TIMING

We have found that on a day's walk the average pace is about 2 miles (3.25 kilometres) per hour. This will include time to 'stand and stare', and time for morning/afternoon breaks and picnic lunch.

DISTANCES

Most people still think in yards and miles, but metres and kilometres will eventually take over. Walking 100 metres or 100 yards along a road to a stile is really no different, but miles and kilometres are vastly different. In the text distances are given in metres, but on the route maps the indication is shown in miles. NB. one kilometre is 5 eighths of a mile, and one mile is 1.6 km (or at least they were when we went to school!).

ORDNANCE SURVEY

Maps seem to be updated about every 20 years, so where a Post Office is marked is no guarantee that it is still there (but there are still some 19000 in the UK!). Also, you will find that some hedges shown on the maps have disappeared or some arrived!

BOTANY

Apart from the sheer joy of being out in the countryside, an enormous number of walkers now have some interest in identifying plant species (ie. herbaceous and tree species). There are some 8500 species to be found in the UK, so the argument for becoming a botanist, as well as a rambler, is quite strong.

Many species restrict themselves to the coast or inland only. Again, whilst many species will be found throughout the walk there are many which will only be found in the south, or only in the north. Happy hunting.

HEDGES

You may recall mathematical laws from years ago. Well, Dr Max Hooper invented Hooper's Rule. The rule is basically that a hedge can be approximately dated from

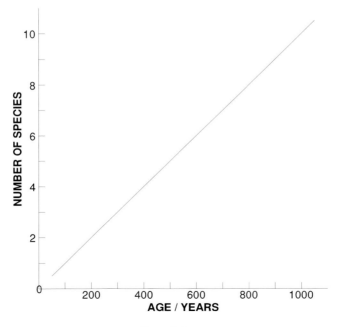

Hooper's Law

the number of tree species in a given distance. Count the number of native species in a 30 yard (or 30 metre) stretch, and consult the chart to find the approximate age when the hedge was first planted.

The trees (or shrubs) which qualify as old native species are—

Alder, Apple, Ash, Beech, Blackthorn, Briar (Dog and Field Rose count as 2), Broom, Buckthorn, Cherry, Cherry Plum, Dogwood, Elder, Elm, Gorse, Guelder Rose, Hawthorn, Hazel, Holly, Hornbeam, Common Lime, Small Leaved Lime, Field Maple, Oak (pedunculate and sessile), Scots Pine, Plum, Poplar, Wild Privet, Rowan, Sallow, Service, Spindle, Sycamore, Wayfaring tree, Whitebeam, Willow (white, crack and goat), and Yew. Identifying hedge ages should give you something to do if you want to add a bit of fun.

LONG DISTANCE PATHS
Along its length the GEW meets Offa's Dyke Path, Wye Valley Way, Shropshire Way, Cestrian Link Walk, Jubilee Way, Staffordshire Way, Sandstone Trail, Mow Cop Trail, Limestone Way, Worcestershire Way, Coast to Coast Path, Reivers Way, Peakland Way, Calderdale Way, Kirklees Way, Weardale Way, Yoredale Way, Ebor Way, Dales Way, Nidderdale Way, and Pennine Way – but not necessarily in that order – and no doubt a number of others also!

HISTORY
Many years ago, when England was made up of a number of Kingdoms like Wessex, Mercia and Northunbria, the Northumbria king, Aethelfrith, came as far south as Chester to win a battle in AD 616. He

must have travelled much the same route as this walk from Northumbria towards Chester.

Years later, in the wars against the Welsh, England built castles at such places as Chepstow, Hereford, Ludlow and Chester. This walk therefore could almost be called 'A Royal Route'.

Much later again, as the Industrial Revolution arrived, many canals were built, and these were followed in turn by railways. The canals and railways were the means to open the country to trade and easier access. Both are given just mention therefore as they are met and crossed on the route.

The oldest building still surviving in most villages and towns is the church. The church usually has all the recorded history and the oldest relics in the area and is an extremely important link with our past.

DISCLAIMER
Things do change. The route described is, as far as is known, all on official rights of way, concessionary or permitted paths. Every effort has been made to ensure the accuracy of the walk, but no responsibility can be accepted for any errors or omissions, or changes to the line of rights of way or concessionary/permitted paths. Walkers should always be aware that adverse weather conditions may make some paths impassable with safety, and should always exercise discretion. County Councils are normally the authority responsible for the maintenance of highways, although some Unitary or Local Authorities have taken on this responsibility. A Public Right Of Way (or PROW) is a right of passage just the same as a road, and many Acts of Parliament have been

Early purple orchid *(Orchis mascula)*

Yellow-rattle *(Rhinantus minor)*

passed over the years to give protection to PROWs. The main Acts date from about 1948 to 1952. The main protection at present for PROW's is probably the Highways Act of 1980.

With so many miles of PROWs it is not surprising that there are some problem paths. The major problems on the route are described in the text (with temporary alternative routes where appropriate), and have been reported to the relevant Highway Authority. Hopefully some of the existing problems may have been solved by the time you do the walk. County Councils only seem to respond to complaints, so do report any problems you find to the relevant County Council.

THE ROUTE

The GEW starts at Chepstow, then goes north (certainly not directly) via the forest of Dean, Malvern Hills, Brown Clee, Wenlock Edge, Caer Caradoc, Shrewsbury, Grinshill, Bickerton Hill, Peckforton Hill, Cheshire Plain, Congleton Edge, Biddulph Moor, Staffordshire Moorlands, Bakewell, Curbar Edge, Hathersage, Derwent Edge, Langsett, Holmfirth, Hebden Bridge, Haworth, Ilkley Moor, Nidderdale, Leyburn, Barnard Castle, Stanhope, Allendale, Vindolanda, Wark, Rothbury, Cheviot Hills, and Wooler to Berwick-upon-Tweed.

TWENTY ONE
Hathersage - Flouch
(20.25 miles or 32.4 km)

Hathersage is a good point to start the second volume, with good transport connexions to Manchester and Sheffield. To leave on the next section, walk along the main road in the Sheffield direction, pass the Hathersage Inn and turn left on Baulk lane. After 200m there is the village cricket pitch on the left. Take the stile on the right, with a sign saying 'To the church'. Follow the right wall and pass through several gates to enter the churchyard of St Michael and All Angels, the parish church of Hathersage. The church possibly dates from as early as the 7th century. Inside the church is a collection of brasses of the Eyre family. Their

graves are at the east end of the churchyard.

Near the church entrance is the grave of 'Little John'. There are 2 stones on the grave—

Here lies buried
Little John
the friend and
Lieutenant of Robin Hood
He died in a cottage (now destroyed)
*   June 24th 1929*
to the east of the churchyard
the grave is marked by

Hathersage from St Michael and All Angels Church

this old headstone and footstone
and is underneath this old Yew tree

The care of this grave
was undertaken by the
Ancient Order
of Foresters Friendly Society

Historical facts are sometimes twisted around in the telling, but there is usually written evidence to confirm the truth. What chance has a legend? A legend is probably based on some actual occurrence, but then changed by the passage of time. The tale which most people know is what has been portrayed in many Hollywood films, where Robin and his merry men are fighting the notorious Sheriff of Nottingham. However, the earlier records of Robin Hood are set in this area and Sherwood is a much later legend (or alteration of the first one). What is known is that there was a large bow and some arrows hanging in the church until about the middle of the 18th century, when they were removed.

The grave of Little John was known and an excavation in 1784 revealed a giant thigh bone. It seems that the original legend is more than likely based on fact. There is an excellent booklet on the subject on sale in the church. There are many places named after Robin Hood in the area – with his well near the Fox House Inn (5 km east), his cave below Stanage Edge (2 km northeast), and the Hood Brook flowing through the village to join the River Derwent being just 3 of the named places. Some 48 km (30 miles) south southwest from here is the village of Doveridge, where Robin proposed

Little John's Grave

to Maid Marian under a Yew tree – which still stands today.

To continue on the interrupted walk, carry on the graveyard path, to exit at the lych gate. Turn left on a minor road until it bends sharp left, and at this point go over a stile on the right, to enter a short green lane. After 100m turn left through a gap near a stone gatepost. Descend 4 steps into a field and follow the left hedge. Cross a stone clapper bridge into the next field, and continue along the hedge. Climb contours to arrive at the next fence line, through which turn half-right to climb to the top left of the field (which is a lovely wild meadow). Go over a stile and follow the left fence, on a level contour, to cross this large field. Pass through another stile at the end, with Brookfield Manor down on the left, and Cowclose Farm ahead. Pass through a gate when you reach the farm buildings, but then bear right around a barn and go through a 2nd gate to drop down to the farm drive (to bypass the farmyard). Proceed along the farm drive to reach a minor road. Turn left on the road for 50m, then right on the drive up to North Lees Hall (thought to have been built in 1594).

The Eyre family, long since disappeared, once owned several houses in the area, including North Lees and Highlow House. Highlow is said to be the most haunted house in Derbyshire (with hauntings recorded from the 14th century). Charlotte Brontë had a holiday in Hathersage in 1845 with her friend Helen Nussey, whose brother was the vicar. She took the Eyre name for her heroine

when she wrote *Jane Eyre* in 1847, and featured North Lees and the village in the book. She stayed in the George Hotel in Hathersage.

Walk along the drive to the right of the house for 100m, then right up 9 steps and through a gate into a field. Cross the centre of the field to reach the right wall (ignore stile going through wall). Continue along the track and over a stile alongside the gate ahead. Follow the enclosed track until you see steps on the left (just before the track reaches a minor road), climb the steps and go over a stile onto the road (to the right of a toilet block).

Turn left on the road for 50m. Go through a gap in the right side wall and head up a clear path towards Stanage Plantation. The path becomes paved and you pass through a gate into the wood, to contin-

North Lees

ue on the paving and exit the wood via another gate. The path now climbs up the Edge. Stanage is a mecca for rock climbers. This is millstone grit rock, a coarse and hard stone. There are probably 500 recognized climbs along this 5 km Edge, and many renowned climbers learnt their craft on these rocks.

Before you reach the top of the Edge turn left to follow the path. [However, should you go a little further, right to the top, then you will see White Path Moss stretching away from you, with the site of Stanedge Pole about 1 km away (the oddity is the spelling of Stanedge Pole against Stanage Edge). The earliest known Peak track is the Roman road from Sheffield via Stanedge Pole to Navio Fort, near Hope,

then via the Snake pass and Doctors Gate to Melandra Camp at Glossop]. The path just below the top soon joins the Long Causeway, the old Roman road. The causeway is now much broken, but walkable. This route was used in the middle ages by 'Jaggers', men who led packhorse trains to and from Sheffield. Follow the old road as it begins to descend (and ignore path going off right after 100m). Continue on this most ancient of routes for a further 400m until it bends left. At this point carry straight on over a stile and along a green path.

This path is also very ancient and was once cobbled in parts. The path must have been part of the route from Hathersage to Strines and northwards. The views west are superb (in good weather!). You soon pass about 100 millstones, of various sizes. The largest is about 6 feet across (just under 2m). The stones were carved by hand on site, using hammer and chisel. They were used mainly for grinding corn, and were often transported to the usage site in pairs on a wooden axle. The stones were sent quite long distances, which clearly increased the price. The death knell was sounded by the import of harder stones from France, and also the increased use of roller mills from the 1860's. The impact of new technology must have been quite severe in such an area.

Over to the northwest can be seen the twin peaks of Win and Lose Hills. There is an unverified legend that about 630AD there was a battle in the area between the King of Northumbria and the King of Wessex. Northumbria won by having possession of the better hill – Win Hill. Strangely Lose Hill is slightly higher than Win Hill.

Carry on along the path through stands of Bracken, and see the Edge to your right diminish, and finally culminate in an outcrop called appropriately Stanage End. The land has now become a Heather moorland. The path bears slightly right towards the 'top' of what is left of the ridge, and Moscar House Farm can be seen ahead on the other side of the valley. The path soon becomes a track and heads off towards a large house, with white gable ends – this is Moscar Lodge on the far side of the road. The track soon brings you to the A57 road. To the west this road is known as the 'Snake Pass', not because of its snake-like route but because the Cavendish family built the 'Snake Inn' in 1821 (named after the snake featured in their coat of arms). The road from Glossop to Sheffield had long been a

Abandoned millstones

packhorse route on the old Roman road, but was made into a proper road in 1821 by Thomas Telford.

Turn left along the road for 600m, then turn right along the road to Strines. You must make a decision at this point. The route over the top of Derwent Edge to Flouch (or Langsett) is long at 24 km/15 miles.   There is an inn and accommodation at Strines, (off the route, at 3.2 km/2 miles north). Only carry on if you have enough time, and acceptable weather.

Walk along the Strines road for 150m, then turn left on the Moscar House Farm drive and pass the house on the left.   Go through a gate and continue for 150m before turning left off the drive along the left bank of the runnel.   Follow the path and cross a plank bridge to keep alongside the right wall. Bear right with the wall and go over a 2nd plank bridge to a stile in a transverse wall. Cross a track (which goes to Moscar House Farm), and follow the track uphill, with a wall now on the left. Pass through a gate and enter open moorland. The track is clear as it climbs, and

Moscar Lodge

121

A57

283

Stanage End

Edge

282

120

crosses the small Highshaw Clough Brook.   50m beyond this you reach grouse butts (No 6) and the track forks. Take the left fork uphill and pass butts numbered 3, 2 and 1. A shooters' track passes over, but keep straight on uphill on this well trodden path.   More butts appear off to the right and you finally reach the summit (at another butt). A public right of way path continues ahead, but turn right here on a NT permissive path to reach the outcrop of rocks called Wheel Stones.   This is Derwent Edge and it has a series of strangely carved millstone grit rocks. There are 3 massive reservoirs down in the valley, but you will not see much of them until you begin to descend to Howden.

Rabbits can be distinguished from hares by having shorter ears (and no black tips to them). They are also smaller, have shorter legs and are an introduced species.   The hare is native to Britain, and we have 2 types – the brown hare which is rare above about 500 metres height, and the mountain hare. The mountain hare is the one you are likely to see in this area, especially in winter when its grey brown coat turns white (except for its black ear tips).   The hen harrier is also likely to be seen up here on the moors.

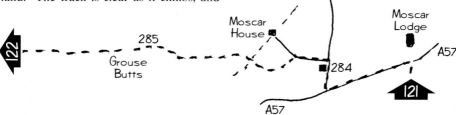

There is now an exhila-
rating walk along the top
of Derwent Edge, which
is surprisingly well visited. The next feature on
the path is White Tor, a large
outcrop of rocks. Looking back
from here the Wheel Stones look like a
coach and horses. Aim north again for
more rocks ahead, and just beyond these
off to the left is perhaps the most well-
known formation. This is the Salt Cellar
(one large boulder). The next point north
is another collection of rocks known as
Dovestone Tor, and just beyond these the
baker has been busy, with 'lumps' of dough

sitting on the moor –
and known as Cakes
of Bread. In this
area the National
Trust have laid
some
paving
stones
to con-
tain ero-
sion.
The
moors are
deep peat
with just a
shallow
cover of
Heather.
Only a slight
usage results in
the peat
breaking up.
You soon
reach a
boundary

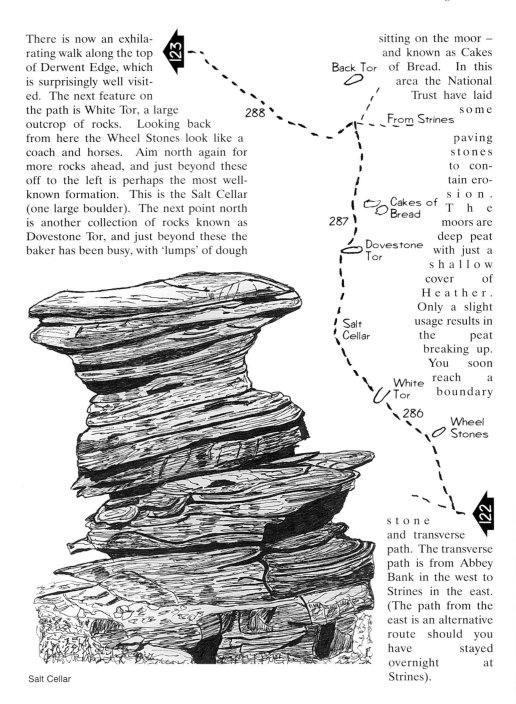

123

288

Back Tor

From Strines

Cakes of Bread

287

Dovestone Tor

Salt Cellar

White Tor

286

Wheel Stones

122

Salt Cellar

stone
and transverse
path. The transverse
path is from Abbey
Bank in the west to
Strines in the east.
(The path from the
east is an alternative
route should you
have stayed
overnight at
Strines).

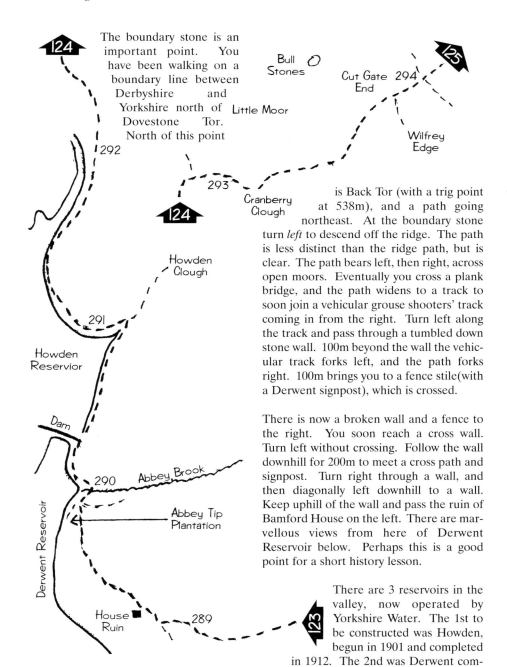

The boundary stone is an important point. You have been walking on a boundary line between Derbyshire and Yorkshire north of Dovestone Tor. North of this point

Bull Stones

Cut Gate 294 End

Little Moor

292

293

Cranberry Clough

Wilfrey Edge

Howden Clough

291

Howden Reservior

Dam

290   Abbey Brook

Abbey Tip Plantation

Derwent Reservoir

House Ruin   289

is Back Tor (with a trig point at 538m), and a path going northeast. At the boundary stone turn *left* to descend off the ridge. The path is less distinct than the ridge path, but is clear. The path bears left, then right, across open moors. Eventually you cross a plank bridge, and the path widens to a track to soon join a vehicular grouse shooters' track coming in from the right. Turn left along the track and pass through a tumbled down stone wall. 100m beyond the wall the vehicular track forks left, and the path forks right. 100m brings you to a fence stile(with a Derwent signpost), which is crossed.

There is now a broken wall and a fence to the right. You soon reach a cross wall. Turn left without crossing. Follow the wall downhill for 200m to meet a cross path and signpost. Turn right through a wall, and then diagonally left downhill to a wall. Keep uphill of the wall and pass the ruin of Bamford House on the left. There are marvellous views from here of Derwent Reservoir below. Perhaps this is a good point for a short history lesson.

There are 3 reservoirs in the valley, now operated by Yorkshire Water. The 1st to be constructed was Howden, begun in 1901 and completed in 1912. The 2nd was Derwent completed in 1916. The 3rd was Ladybower, begun in 1935, and completed in 1943. It was officially opened after the war in September 1945 by King George VI. This reservoir involved the inundation of the villages of Derwent and Ashopton.

During World War II many daring raids took place before the opening of the 2nd front in Normandy in June 1944. One famous air raid was the attack on the Ruhr dams. Sir Barnes Wallis, the famous scientist, devised a bouncing bomb which could be dropped behind a dam wall to create an 'earthquake' effect and shatter a dam.

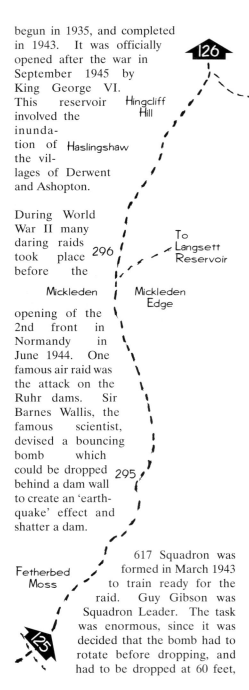

617 Squadron was formed in March 1943 to train ready for the raid. Guy Gibson was Squadron Leader. The task was enormous, since it was decided that the bomb had to rotate before dropping, and had to be dropped at 60 feet,

and at a set distance from the dam (depending on the individual dam being attacked), and also this had to be done at a set air speed (210 mph). Three dams were to be attacked and English dams were chosen as 'look-alikes' for practice. Eyebrook Reservoir was chosen for the Möhne, Abberton for Eder, and Derwent for Sorpe. There were many problems during training, and Derwent was the place where one piece of essential apparatus was proven (how do you judge accurate distance from the dam towers? – answer, use 2 pieces of wood fastened together to form 2 sides of a triangle. Fix a nail in the 2 ends and a peephole at the joint. When the 2 towers line up with the nails you are at the correct distance from the towers to drop the bomb!). The raid took place on the Ruhr in the early hours of 28th May 1943 and the pilots were successful in breaching both the Möhne and the Eder. The Sorpe was unfortunately only slightly damaged. A commemoration flight by a Lancaster bomber was made over the dam in 1993, watched by thousands of spectators.

Keep uphill of the wall as you walk along. Derwent Reservoir and its dam towers are very clear. The wall swings left as Howden Reservoir comes into view and you follow it to descend steeply towards the upper reaches of Derwent Reservoir. Abbey Tip plantation wood is entered through a wall, and then exited onto a forest road. Turn right on the 'road' and go over the bridge of Abbey Brook. There is now a long easy walk along the reservoir.

Ignore a path going off to the left to the dam base and continue on the 'road'. This stretch is well used by mountain bikers at weekends, but they don't go far up the valley-since they are usually on a circular trip around the reservoirs. Continue up to and past the dam of Howden Reservoir. You pass a 'bay' of the reservoir, and continue around the corner of the bay to reach an area called Cold Side, where the track forks. Take the right fork to enter the NT area of Derwent estate. The path does not stray far from the water. As the reservoir ends you walk along the infant River Derwent and arrive at a bridge on the left. This is a 17th century packhorse bridge. Originally the bridge was in the village of Derwent Woodlands (flooded when the Ladybower was opened). It was demolished before the reservoir opened and rebuilt here in 1959.

Carry on the track to pass the bridge and cross a footbridge over Cranberry Clough Brook. The path bears right and starts to climb. Soon there is a fork, take the right fork and enter the NT land of Howden Moor. Walk up Cranberry Clough with the stream to your right and cross Stony Bank Clough Beck. The path now begins a tortuous climb up several hundred man made steps.

At the top pause for breath and then continue climbing the path, but more gradually. Ahead to the left is the rock outcrop of Bull Stones. Names mean little in this vast space, but as you climb you see (slightly right) a ridge. This is Wilfrey Edge, and the highest point of this is graced with the name of Margery Hill at 546m (*Abdon Burf was only 540m).

You meet a NT pavement again for a short stretch. The path goes through a 'pass' in the slight ridge and across a transverse path. Continue to follow the clear path marked by a few cairns at this point. The horizon is featureless until suddenly you see windmills a long way ahead! As you continue you are rewarded at last by the sight of houses and green pastures in the far distance. A spring gives rise to a small beck, which slowly becomes a depression and then a valley to your left. The beck is Mickleden Beck, and you become aware that you are walking on a small edge – Mickleden Edge. The path reaches a fork marked by a footpath sign. The sign is iron

Erosion

and was erected by the Peak and Northern Footpaths Society in 1925. The society is the oldest footpath group, having been formed in 1894 (the Ramblers' Association itself was formed in 1935). The signpost is of more than passing interest since it points the way ahead to Flouch and Hazlehead Station. The line closed in the 1970's.

Carry on ahead to shortly go through a broken wall, and then continue across moorland. There is a small ridge to cross called

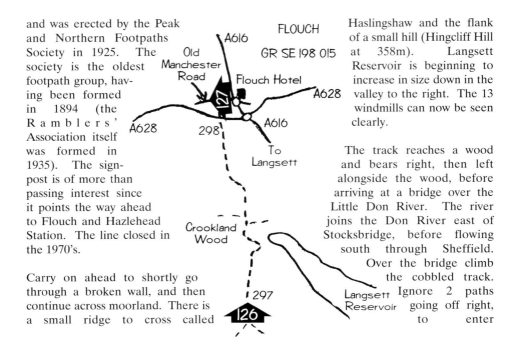

Haslingshaw and the flank of a small hill (Hingcliff Hill at 358m). Langsett Reservoir is beginning to increase in size down in the valley to the right. The 13 windmills can now be seen clearly.

The track reaches a wood and bears right, then left alongside the wood, before arriving at a bridge over the Little Don River. The river joins the Don River east of Stocksbridge, before flowing south through Sheffield. Over the bridge climb the cobbled track. Ignore 2 paths going off right, to enter

Old signpost

Crookland Wood. Some 250m brings you to another fork and another Peak and Northern footpath sign (marked to the Flouch Inn). Turn *left* here off the track and down to a footpath. The path bears right after 100m to follow a left wall. Exit the wood and walk up to the A628 bypass road (with a Barnsley MBC footpath sign). Cross the road to continue on the woodland path. After 70m cross a stile to walk on the right of a wall and reach the original main road, now a cut off cul-de-sac. Turn right to reach the small roundabout and the Flouch which stands at 289m.

The Flouch has been an inn ever since anyone can remember, and was well known as one of the "Pass Inn's". These were inns which in the olden days offered a point of succour when the roads became blocked by snow. The Snake Inn on the A57 was a similar place. Time marches on, and the M62 now offers an alternative route over the Pennines. The final straw for the Flouch was obviously when the bypass was built. The inn became a Country Cantonese Restaurant. You will be pleased to know that the Flouch still offers accommodation along with meals. An alternative would be to divert from the path to Langsett, which has a shop, inn with accommodation and a youth hostel. Then return to the path to reach this point.

TWENTY TWO
Flouch - Holmfirth
(8.75 miles or 14.0 km)

The country north of Flouch is less wild, so hasten ye onwards. From the Flouch Hotel cross the small roundabout and retrace your steps to the point where the footpath from the south meets the old Manchester road. Carry on west on the cul-de-sac road and pass an old milestone announcing that it is 13 miles to Barnsley and 23 miles to Manchester. The road carries on to almost meet the new A628 road, but just before this point are some cottages on the right. Turn right between White Cottages and Acre Head Cottage on a signposted bridleway.

The route is initially a walled green track, with walled fields to both sides. The windmill farm, with its 13 'mills' is now very clear to the northeast. Pass through a gate and leave the fields behind to cross Low Moor. Fortunately there is still a wall to your right to guide the way. Ordnance Survey maps show the path to the right of the wall, but these are incorrect – the route is to the left of the wall. A long straight walk brings you

to a gate with a house over to the right side. Bear left with the wall which takes you to Cote Bank Bridge and cross the old railway line.

The line used to be one of the most important in the country, being the main line across the Pennines from Manchester to Sheffield. Fast trains would stop at Guide Bridge and Penistone only en-route and took 1 hour 5 minutes. However, the timetable for stopping trains was much slower eg. leave Manchester London Road (long since renamed Piccadilly) at 3.52pm, Guide Bridge 4.07, Godley Junction 4.17, Dinting 4.27 (with a change of train to carry on to Glossop, arrive 4.38), Hadfield 4.31, Crowden 4.40, Woodhead 4.46, Dunford Bridge 4.53, Hazlehead Bridge 4.58, Penistone 5.04, Wortley 5.14, Deepcar 5.17, Oughty Bridge 5.23, Wadsley Bridge 5.28, Neepsend 5.32, Sheffield Victoria 5.35.

GR SE 198 015

You will recall that the old Peak and Northern footpath signs south of Flouch were signposted Flouch and Hazlehead station. The line was so important that it was the first main line to be electrified overhead in the United Kingdom...in 1954. Shortly after this British Rail decided to close the line (about 1970 to passengers and about 1981 to freight), and make the route from Manchester via Edale and Hathersage to Sheffield into the main line. After all these years the rail line is now partly used for walking and cycling.

Having crossed the railway bridge go through a gate and turn half-left down a flagged path leading to a wide earth track. Turn left on the track and almost immediately right to cross a footbridge over the River Don. The river goes on to be the main river flowing through Sheffield. Turn right over the bridge to cross a 2nd bridge and then left on a walled green lane, to reach Soughley

(a large farm, with very large barn doors – perhaps the horses used to be very tall in these parts!) and a tarmac road. Turn left over the bridge and cross the Town Brook, onto a green track for 70m to reach 2 gates. Pass through either gate and turn half-right to pass a brick chamber. Head uphill to the top far left field corner. These are the green fields you saw from the moors south of Flouch. Go over a stile and continue the same line to a stile 30m short of the top left field corner. Through this stile follow the wall on the right . The outlook to the left, on a dull day, is of desolate moorland. You reach a point where the wall turns right, and a farm track joins from the left. Turn right on the track, pass through a gate and then follow the track left.

The grounds of Carlecotes Hall are over the wall to the right. The track swings right, and just past this point is a stile on the right. Go over the stile into a sunken walled path to reach the church of St Anne. The church was obviously built as the private church for the hall, but is now a public church with regular services. Pass by on the path and through a carved church gate to reach the 'hamlet'. A

Barn at Soughley Farm

hamlet is a village without a church. Carlecotes has a church, but only about 12 houses/farms – does this make it a village? Turn left on the road and pass the old 1830 school house. As you walk along the road the small wooded valley of the River Don opens out down on your left with Townhead hamlet. There are also glimpses of traffic on the mid horizon on the A628 Woodhead road. The 221m (725 feet) high TV mast at Holme Moss comes into view. This was the first TV mast to be built in the north of England. There are fields on your right, which give way to a short stretch of open moor. A wall goes off to the right. 100m beyond this is a bus stop and a bridleway sign at an old small quarry. Turn right on this path, initially following a wall. Turn right with the wall and over a stile after 70m. Follow the wall until it turns right again (to return to the road), at which point you should turn left for 20m, then turn half-right through the tussocks of grass to cross Topping Moor.

Initially head just left of the large chimney (marked Hepworth) which can be seen in the distance. There are some blue pole markers en-route, the first of which is to the right of a small fenced-off area. You see a stone wall coming in from the right, aim for a point 100m left of this wall (still aiming for the chimney). A 2nd blue pole marker is passed and you should now head for a transverse wall ahead. The Hepworth works buildings are now becoming very clear. Hepworths was originally an iron

works and was served by a branch line from the main railway, but is now a vitrified clay products' works. When you reach the wall turn left to follow it for some 150m until it turns right. Follow the wall round to the right for 100m to 2 plank bridges (a stile goes off right), and then turn left with the wall for 150m to a gate. Follow the wall on the right (again OS maps show path on opposite wall side) and through 2 gates onto Flint Lane.

Turn left on the lane and climb up to the Foxhouse Inn and restaurant at the hamlet of Knowles. The lane soon arrives at a crossroads. Turn right on Beddingedge road for 250m to reach 2 semi detached houses on the left. Just past the houses is a bus stop on the right and a stile on the left. Go over the stile to leave South Yorkshire and enter West Yorkshire county. Initially follow the left wall, then get over a broken wall/fence where in 1997 the stile was missing. Go forward for 50m to find an old green track. This is an old mining area and there is an old slagheap/loading area on the right. You quickly reach a transverse broken wall and descend the track (ignore track going off right). Keep an old wall to the left. The small hill to the right has a name...Crow Hill. Keep following the broken wall downhill to reach an old signpost just before 2 buildings at Ox Lee (an abandoned quality farmhouse).

Turn left to enter the old farm track and pass the ruined farm. The track was obviously of good construction and initially paved – at least in parts. The route is muddy at first, but soon climbs to drier ground and also has the name of Ox Lee Lane. Follow the clear lane to reach a tarmac minor road (Far Lane). Go straight across onto Cowcliff Hill Road. The solitary windmill seen ahead is at Longley Farm, and is used to generate power for their famous dairy products. (yogurts, cream etc).

CLIFF

130

307

HOLMFIRTH
GR SE 142 082

NEW GATE

Housing Estate

306

SCHOLES

305

Morton Woods

129 Wood

Pass 1 stile on the right and then a road to reach a small wood on the right (Morton Wood). The wood ends, but just before you reach Jordan House turn right over a stone stile to skirt the wood. Follow the right wall and the wood ends after the 2nd stile, but still follow the right wall and another field brings you to 48 steps going down to a walled defile. The way opens out to arrive at an unmetalled road. Turn right before a house for 20m. Then *right* again onto a wooden staircase going down to a permissive path alongside New Mill Dike (in other words a stream).

There is now a most delightful walk through Morton

Path into Morton Wood

Wood (this is also part of the Kirklees Way walk). There are a lot of Beech trees initially, which means beech mast (the nut of the tree) underfoot. This is a food much loved by squirrels. The wood stretches for over a kilometre, with the path following the route of the dike. There are a number of wooden footbridges and huge stepping stones to cross as the path weaves from one side of the dike to the other. At one point there is a shale cliff on the right side, and a smaller one on the left with a fine collection of Ferns (Hard and Broad Buckler). There is also Great Wood-rush in this area. Pink Purslane gives a splash of colour later in the year. Eventually the wood thins and you reach a stile to pass through gardens on each side and onto the road. (In the *Last of the Summer Wine 'Stop That Bath'* episode, the runaway bath came down the hill to your right).

Turn left on the road and pass more picturesque houses and gardens as you climb. At the hill top there is a road junction – keep left on Chapelgate to enter Scholes village.

Scholes is an old village, and is surrounded by windswept Scholes Moor. Much of the village is built of millstone grit. The late Roy Castle was born in the village.

Walk along Chapelgate for 150m, then turn left along a farm lane (opposite Marsh Road). Continue along the lane for 450m, passing the cricket club and football pitch to right and left en route. Turn right on a tarmac road and follow this to a cross road. Cross over onto Cross Lane and pass a new housing estate on the right. Carry on to pass Ryecroft Lane on the right. The lane soon bends left, at which point you should turn right on an access road (with a few cottages). The 'road' quickly becomes a narrow track with extensive views down to Holmfirth, and is a very good ridge walk. 450m on the track brings you to a fork, take the left track heading downhill towards a housing estate and meet a minor road. Opposite is a path, which although not marked as a footpath on the map, is clearly

well used. Cross the road onto the track passing to the left of lock-up garages and skirt the housing estate (passing the ends of 2 roads on the way). The path is narrow, but brings you to a rugby pitch on the other side of the estate. At the far side of the pitch are 3 public rights of way...all walled tracks. One goes ahead, one right, and one goes left just beyond the pitch – this is the one to follow. The path soon becomes a tarmaced drive leading to Cinderhills Road. Turn right on the road, which soon bears left and becomes South Lane. The lane leads downhill to join Dunford Road and onto Holmfirth centre.

There used to be regular train services from Brockholes (on the Huddersfield to Sheffield line) to Holmfirth. The journey time was 6 minutes, but the line closed many years ago.

Inside Ivy's Café Holmfirth, reproduced by kind permission of Mr Colin Frost of Sid's Café. The café was used in Last of the Summer Wine.

Holy Trinity church dates from 1472 (then a chapelry in the parish of Kirkburton), but the present Georgian church dates from 1782, being rebuilt after the flood damage of 1777 (with the tower added in 1788). The town has an excellent choral society, whose conductor in 1857 was Joe Perkins, who arranged Pratty Flowers, known as the Holmfirth anthem.

The town's development is linked to textiles. Moorland sheep and fast flowing streams provided an ideal setting for the industry. There are still many mill sites to be seen, and weavers' cottages. The area produced, and still does, some of the finest woollen yarns and cloths. Local firms supply materials to some of the top names in the fashion world. From Holmfirth centre narrow ginnels (passageways) climb up to weavers' hamlets, and the area begs further exploration if you have the time. There is also a postcard museum in the town.

There is no doubt that Holmfirth today is best known however for the TV series *'Last of the Summer Wine'*. The programme has run for some 26 years and anyone who has seen the programme (which must surely be everyone in the land!), cannot fail to know the names of Compo, Clegg, Foggy, Nora, Ivy, Howard, Marina, and many more. The programme is the longest running comedy series in the World! Sid's cafe is in the town centre and serves ordinary people as well as celebrities with refreshments. Nora Batty and Compo's houses are just 5 minutes walk away , and much of the town centre will be recognisable from the series. A film was also made of the series. The 'local' pub used in the series is the *'White Horse Inn'* on Scholes Road at Jackson Bridge (0.5 km east of Scholes village).

Ivy's Café Holmfirth

TWENTY THREE
Holmfirth - Ripponden
(15.0 miles or 24.0 km)

Leave on Towngate (if you follow this road to the left you can visit Nora and Compo's houses), and turn right over the River Holme bridge, where a plaque records floods of 1852 and 1944, with 81 and 3 lives lost respectively. Walk up Victoria Street and turn right onto Huddersfield Road for 50m, then left up the very steep Cooper Lane.

In the word's of Sir Ben Turner—

Its nice to ramble up be't Ford
Or trail oe'r Cartworth Moor
And yer t'lark sing his melody
For all, boeth rich and poor

At a T junction turn right on Holt Lane for 20m, then head left (before No 1) to climb

the path and steps.
The path emerges on a tarmac lane called 'Hill'. Turn left and the route quickly becomes a walled earth track (there are numerous walled tracks in this area leading to the old weaving hamlets of the valley). The track bends between fields to arrive at a road at the delightful hamlet of Upperthong. Cross the road and walk along Towngate, passing the old Weavers House and Royal Oak Inn to reach a T junction at Wickens Lane. Turn left down Broad Lane for 50m, then go over the stile opposite No 100. Head across the centre of

the large field to a 2nd stone stile, then cross a small field and once over the 3rd stile follow the left wall for a further field. A path splits off left, but keep following the left wall through 2 further fields, to cross a stile putting the wall to your right. 50m brings a stile switching the path and putting you back with a left wall. Cross 3 further small fields to arrive at a 'ruined' farmhouse.

At this point there is a choice, either pass in front of the house and turn right on an access track and follow it as it bends right and left, or bypass by turning 45 degrees right before the house to reach the track behind the house. Emley Moor TV aerial is now over to the east, and Holme Moss aerial to the south as you walk to the metalled Dean Road. Emley Moor TV mast is the tallest free standing man-made structure in Europe at over 1200 feet (365m) tall. The trig point can be seen on Wolfstones Height (325m) just northeast. Turn left along the road to The Ford Inn at a road junction. Turn right on Thick Hollins Road for 300m to a gate on the left (passing Bradshaw Road going off right along the way). Go through the gate and follow the left wall through 6 fields to reach Harden Hill Farm. Pass left of the house and onto the unmade

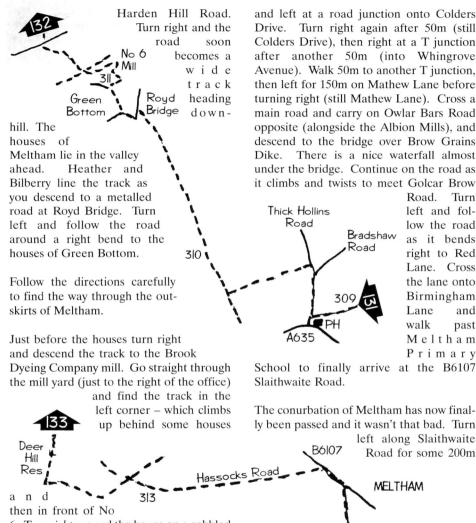

Harden Hill Road. Turn right and the road soon becomes a wide track heading down-hill. The houses of Meltham lie in the valley ahead. Heather and Bilberry line the track as you descend to a metalled road at Royd Bridge. Turn left and follow the road around a right bend to the houses of Green Bottom.

Follow the directions carefully to find the way through the out-skirts of Meltham.

Just before the houses turn right and descend the track to the Brook Dyeing Company mill. Go straight through the mill yard (just to the right of the office) and find the track in the left corner – which climbs up behind some houses and then in front of No 6. Turn *right* around the house on a cobbled lane for 30m, then hairpin left onto a ter-raced path. Go along the terrace for 100m, then sharp right on a path up through a Gorse thicket and rocks to reach an unmade road. Cross the road onto another unmade walled road and reach a tarmaced minor road. Cross this road and continue on a walled track for 100m, then turn right on a track which soon becomes metalled,

and left at a road junction onto Colders Drive. Turn right again after 50m (still Colders Drive), then right at a T junction after another 50m (into Whingrove Avenue). Walk 50m to another T junction, then left for 150m on Mathew Lane before turning right (still Mathew Lane). Cross a main road and carry on Owlar Bars Road opposite (alongside the Albion Mills), and descend to the bridge over Brow Grains Dike. There is a nice waterfall almost under the bridge. Continue on the road as it climbs and twists to meet Golcar Brow Road. Turn left and fol-low the road as it bends right to Red Lane. Cross the lane onto Birmingham Lane and walk past Meltham Primary School to finally arrive at the B6107 Slaithwaite Road.

The conurbation of Meltham has now final-ly been passed and it wasn't that bad. Turn left along Slaithwaite Road for some 200m

Near Deer Hill Reservoir

and then left into Hassocks Road, which very quickly becomes a walled track. Pass over the massive bridge of Catchwater Drain. Deer Hill is ahead and the hill of Meltham Cop is behind. Skylarks are hard to find in the agricultural areas in the south, but they are heard aplenty up here on the moors in spring. The left wall ends and the track carries on with a right side wall only, to join another earth road

Huddersfield
Narrow Canal

River
Colne

A62

PH

315

B6107

314

Deer Hill
Reservoir

(Deer Hill End Road). Turn left for 150m, then branch right on the access road to Deer Hill Reservoir. Turn right along the Water Board road and then left at the end to go along the dam side. Continue to the end. Swing left to cross the reservoir overflow bridge and onto the old reservoir keeper's house. Directly opposite the house is a car parking spot and out of this is a gate leading to a

track across Lingards Wood Moor. The track is stone lined and possibly an old packhorse trail across the moors. The track descends to a bridge over Blackmoorfoot Conduit, and swings left and right down to the B6107 (Meltham Road). Turn left on the road for 25m, then right down a narrow lane leading to Hill Farm dated 1616.

Negotiate the farm by passing between a barn to the left and house to the right, and onto yet another walled track for a short distance to join a transverse walled track (part of the Colne Valley circular walk). Turn right over a stile for 50m to a path junction. Take the little used left fork which brings you to the left side of a row of houses and over a stile onto the A62.

Turn left for 50m to just before the Olive Branch Inn, turning into the inn car park. At the left back of the car park is a gate giving access to a tarmac path across a field to a bridge over a small canal cut to serve Holme Mill, then over the River Colne and onto the towpath of the Huddersfield Narrow Canal.

The Act of Parliament authorising the canal construction was passed in 1794. The canal is 19.75 miles long, and has 74 locks, 5 aqueducts and 3 tunnels, and opened in 1811. The canal runs from the Ashton Canal at Portland Basin, Ashton-under-Lyne to Huddersfield (birthplace of that wonderful actor James Mason and of the Labour Prime Minister Sir Harold Wilson). The last commercial traffic was in 1935 and the canal was culverted through part of Stalybridge in the 1960's. The canal, being narrow, only allowed boats of up to 6 foot 1 inch (185cm) to pass. The canal has the longest tunnel on any canal, Standedge at 3.25 miles (5.2 km), and is also the highest canal at 645 feet (196m). There is no towpath through the tunnel and boats were 'legged' through. The tunnel is 2.5 km west of this point and last saw a boat passage in 1963 by the famous L T C Rolt. The good news however is that the Millenium Commission has made a large monetary award towards restoration of the canal in 2000. A heritage centre is also planned for the Marsden tunnel end.

The navigators or 'navvies' who built the canals were a hardy bunch about whom much has been written, and the following anonymous poem perhaps explains some of their feelings—

I am a navvy bold, thats trampelled the county round, sir,

to get a job of work
where any can be found, sir,
I left my native home
my friends and my relations
to ramble up and down
and work in various stations

Chorus:-

I'm a navvy don't you see
I'm a navvy in my prime
I'm a nipper, I'm a tipper
and I'm working on the line.
At Colne I worked a fortnight
before it came to pay day
we went into the town
the jug went quickly round, sir,
we all got very drunk and spent full many a crown, sir.

Turn right on the towpath for 20m and then left over lock 31 bridge. Follow the access

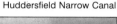
Huddersfield Narrow Canal

track to go under the railway bridge (the Manchester to Huddersfield line via Ashton and Stalybridge). Beyond the bridge is a cross road which is crossed to climb the path opposite.

The path is an alternative stream! but follow the right wall uphill until there is a gap on the right (the track ahead becomes blocked) and at this point go diagonally right. Booth Naze Hill is now to the left at 275m. Follow the right wall up a track to reach a house, but just before the house turn left up the hill to a stile in the top wall. Over the stile cross the field to a wall corner (slightly right), go over a stile and follow a rightside wall to drop down to a minor road. Turn right on the road, which is lined with Coltsfoot in spring. There is a TV repeater station ahead on Cop Hill. After 300m the road turns sharp right. At this point you should turn left onto a green track and climb Cop Hill to reach a minor road.

Cross the road onto an earth road for 70m only, then left over a stile near 2 small houses. Keep to the right of the houses across a field to another stile, then in the next field keep height – but follow an obvious ridge across the field and swing left with it at the far side. There is now a junction of fences and walls. Turn left and right to follow a fence across a small field to reach a stile and Coal Gate Road.

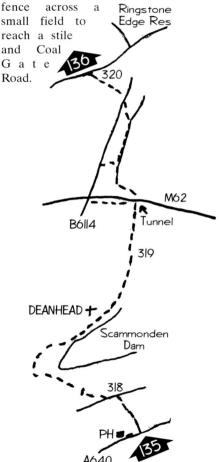

Turn right on the road and follow it around a bend (where it changes name to Bradshaw Lane) to reach Newgate Farm. Opposite the farm turn left up a track and follow the right wall through 2 fields. The path then goes over a stile to swop to the left wall side for 1 field, then follows a fence to pass left of a farm. Continue uphill to pass right of another house and onto unmade Burnt Plats Lane. Cross over and follow a right fence for 100m, then pass through this and keep it about 50m to your left to pass through a wall stile. Head straight for the A640 road and the famous Nont Sarah's Inn. The inn has always been known as a stopping place on the Pennine crossing from Denshaw, especially in bad weather. The inn is at 1168 feet (356m).

The inn has a marvellous view of Scammonden Water, a reservoir created when the M62 motorway was built. The reservoir dam wall forms the motorway, which can now be clearly seen, but fortunately is hidden behind embankments to each side and therefore does not *yet* create much noise.

Turn right on the road for 100m then left down a green road (Redgate Lane) to meet a metalled road. Cross diagonally left (signposted Scammonden Sailing Club) and go down the road until it turns sharp right, at which point you carry straight on to pass over a plank footbridge. Bear half-right to descend to a footbridge over Black Burne Brook. Turn half-right up the hillside then aim for the church ahead at Deanhead. The path passes about 70m below the church on a beautiful wood/moor walk. The path is well defined, but noise from the

motorway becomes louder as the church is passed. The path keeps more or less on the same contour, *do not* climb up to the road above. As the motorway dam wall is reached there is a tunnel ahead passing below the motorway, beyond which is a track turning left up to a minor road (Scammonden Road). At the tunnel there is also a footpath signpost pointing west up to a metalled road leading to the B6114 road, which is followed over the M62 before turning right down a track to the aforementioned Scammonden Road.

Having arrived at Scammonden Road turn north to pass some houses, then a line of trees each side as you pass over Hey House Clough and Stream. 30m beyond this point leave the road via a left gate and head diagonally right up the field to reach the B6114 road. Turn right for 30m then (opposite a T junction) go left on a path into Clock Face Wood and cross over a transverse path after 5m. The path has now been moved around a quarry extension ahead, but the path is clear as you walk around to the right of the quarry face and Ringstone Edge Reservoir appears to your right (and the motorway noise ends as you cross over the rise). Head across the Heather moor and down to a minor road. Turn left on the road for 10m then take a right fork onto Cockpit Lane.

Cock fighting was always illegal but must have been carried on here in the past for this lane to earn its name. Carry on down the lane to reach Cockpit Farm. The track now becomes a walled path (Rishworth can be seen on the opposite valley side). After 200m the walled track turns left and you leave it through a stile on the right heading straight downhill, following a left fence to arrive at the end of a minor road. Spread Eagle House is on the left. Turn sharp right down unmade Heys Lane (yet another walled track), and after 70m go over a footbridge and turn left (ignore the 2 footpaths going straight ahead) and climb up the track. Pass a ruined house to the left and 100m further on turn left along a narrow walled track. Descend to a path junction. Turn right on a level bridleway for 200m until the left wall ends. Turn left to descend to the old railway bridge (there used to be a line from Sowerby Bridge to Ripponden and onwards to serve works south of the town). The bridge is still intact over the overgrown line and there are 39 steps down from the bridge to reach the River Ryburn (the main tributary of the River Calder).

Do not cross the river bridge but turn right along the bank and pass a few houses.

Enter the playing fields and walk to the left side to exit and go along an old lane between houses. Go under the bridge of Greetland Road to reach Priest Lane and the parish church of St Bartholomew, the 4th on this site-built in 1868; the first church being built in 1464. Turn left on the packhorse bridge. The first bridge is recorded in 1313, with a more substantial one being built in 1533 for 7/6d. The present bridge dates from 1772 and has a 52 foot (nearly 16m) span. Ripponden is a meeting place of several ancient routes and was a convenient fording place over the river (the ancient name of the village was *Rybourndene* meaning *A Ford over a River in a Valley*). Pass the Old Bridge Inn, probably Yorkshire's oldest hostelry – earliest recorded date 1307 but thought to be much older, and go up cobbled Priest Lane to the A58 road.

Disused rail line at Ripponden

St Bartholomew Church and Priest Lane Ripponden

TWENTY FOUR
Ripponden - Hebden Bridge
(8.0 miles or 12.8 km)

From the junction of Priest Lane with the A58 turn left for a few metres then right up Back Lane. The lane soon changes name to Spring Street (with a bank full of Bistort) and then bear right up Ripponden Old Lane. The lane climbs past sparse houses to reach a cross road. Cross the road and continue on the same line for a further 100 m before turning right on a walled track. 2 more tracks go off at right angles, but keep going forward until you reach a T junction. Turn left onto this walled track (Cote Road) to pass Low Cote Farm, built in 1671 and now restored to its former glory. Just beyond the farm take a right fork to arrive at metalled Green Lane. Cross over and pass Star Cottage on the left. After 100m turn right through a gate before a stone barn, going downhill with a wall to the left. Pass through well-worn stiles to the minor road at Wells Bottom.

Cross the road and go along the very wide earth road opposite. There is a junction of paths after 400m – going left, right, and straight ahead. Take the middle route straight ahead, keeping on this main path, flagged in parts, to swing right to Far Slack Farm. Enter the farmyard and turn left before the farmhouse to exit onto yet another walled track. The route north from Holmfirth has been marked by ancient walled tracks and unmade roads.

When the left wall ends, stay with the right wall, following it as it swings right to a gated stile. Pass through the stile and follow the low wall to the right as you walk across the flank of Great Manshead Hill (summit 1 km west at 404m). A footbridge is reached at the head of Blackshaw Clough. Climb

RIPPONDEN
GR SE 040 197

50m beyond this point and turn right through a gate. Cross to the wall on the left and follow it to meet a sunken track and a windmill and Greave Head Farm.

Go through a gate to the left of the farmhouse and along the drive to Coal Gate Road (these road names keep repeating themselves!). Turn right on the road for 30m, then off left on the unmade Greave Head Road. Follow the right wall to old quarry workings. The wall changes to the left side, then right again and ends at a path junction. Continue ahead on the well-defined track to pass more old workings and cross a transverse path (the Calderdale Way). A left wall is now followed down the old cobbled quarry roadway which soon

138
Far Slack
324

Wells Bottom

Low Cote
323

Star Cottage

Ripponden Old Road

A58

A692

322 137

bears right on a farm access road. After 150m tracks go off left and right but carry on descending. A further 100m brings more path junctions. Turn left with the farm road to descend to New Road.

Cross over a stile opposite and descend through a field with a wall to the left to reach an electricity pole. Go over the nearby stile into a watery track and down to the left of 2 farmhouses to reach the B6138 road.

Turn right on the road (passing Moorland Cottages) for about 150m, then descend steps on the left, to the side of No. 6 Cragg Road. The path veers behind the houses and down into Torvin Clough to an old clapper bridge over Cragg Brook. This is an area full of the sound of rushing water. Turn right along the brook, then follow the path as it takes higher ground into a beautiful Birch wood. The path goes through to the left of the wood and meets an unmade road. Turn right for 100m to a minor road then right again to pass (or stop for a drink) the Hinchcliffe Arms Inn at Marshaw Bridge.

Turn left before the bridge onto a track between the inn and its car park, then pass Cragg Vale Tennis Club. The path begins to climb as rocks now tower above the brook, and as the track forks take the left one to continue upwards and through 2 stiles

Ancient stile near Wells Bottom

to the left of a house garden. The path now runs parallel with a minor access road and then breaks onto the road. Turn left on this minor road and ignore paths going off left and right, then turn left between 2 houses and through the gate at the back. Pass left of a stable in the field and follow the right wall uphill. Go over a stile and then follow the left wall/fence as it bears left. At the field end more paths cross, but carry on uphill to the left of a wall to a gate onto an unmade road at High Green Farm.

Turn right for a few metres then over an indistinct stone stile on the left opposite the farmhouse. Head diagonally right to the far field corner, going over a stile onto Bell House Moor. Keep on the same direction to reach Keelham Farm. Calder Valley and Mytholmroyd can now be clearly seen (in good weather!). At the farm bear left on an access track and follow the right wall. The track leads down to Bell House, but *do not* lose height. Well before reaching the house an ancient flagged path goes off left to head across the moor. The flags are missing in parts, giving a very wet walk across a number of flushes to reach the head of the ravine of Spring Wood, with spectacular views down to the valley. At the head of the ravine the path splits. Take the right fork to keep around the top of the drop and in 100m the path splits again. A path goes right down the ravine and to Mytholmroyd (birthplace of Poet Laureate Ted Hughes), but the GEW keeps to the left path at this point to reach a tumble-down wall.

Follow the left side of what remains of the wall across the moor and arrive at a cross wall (still standing).

Wall at Greave Head Road

Clapper bridge over Cragg Brook

Go left along the wall to reach the left corner, and turn half-right to head downhill. Cross a brook and keep left of another wall corner to find a stile in a transverse wall. Hebden Bridge is now clearly seen below. Go over the stile and down on, or to the left of, an old collapsed walled track – to meet an unmade road. Turn left on the 'road' and soon pass Moorside Farm and 'The Hawthorns', to reach Great Jumps farmhouse. Go through the farmyard and follow the farm access road round to the right, then left and over a cattle grid. Turn left to pass left of Old Chamber Farm. Go past disused farm workers' cottages and turn right on a path in the gap between 2 barns, over a stile into a field. Cross diagonally left to a stile, keeping on the same line through several fields and stiles, to enter Crow Nest Wood. Follow the track through the wood, over a transverse track, following the same line (and later a wall to the right). On leaving the wood the track becomes metalled, then unmetalled again. Keep on the same direction until a bend right brings you to a road.

Turn left, through traffic lights, and cross the railway bridge (over the Manchester, Rochdale and Halifax line). Follow the road left after the bridge for 30m then turn right down steps, and left to reach the Rochdale Canal at a point where the canal has an aqueduct over the River Calder.

When we went to school we were taught in Geography lessons about the rivers of Yorkshire, and learnt the word SUNWAC. These are the rivers of Yorkshire from north to south. Well the GEW is going north, therefore the first letter it reaches is 'C' for Calder. The rivers Aire, Wharfe, Nidd, Ure and Swale are still to come.

The Rochdale Canal was the first of the 3 trans-Pennine canals to be completed (the other 2 being Huddersfield Narrow and Leeds-Liverpool). First surveys were done by James Brindley, and later surveys and work were done by John Rennie. After many upsets the canal was finally opened in 1798 from Sowerby Bridge to Rochdale, and extended to Manchester in 1804. The canal is 33 miles (53Km) in length and has 92 locks. It links the Calder and Hebble navigation at Sowerby Bridge with the Ashton and Bridgewater in Manchester.

Once on the towpath turn right and then left over the canal bridge

HEBDEN BRIDGE
GR SD 992 271

141
A6033
330
A646
Crow Nest Wood
Old Chamber
Great Jumps
329 Moorside Farm
Erringden Moor
Spring Ravine
328
Bell House
Keelham
Bell House Moor
High Green
140

to reach Hebden Bridge centre.

Hebden Bridge is a former mill town which was originally a river crossing point in medieval times. There is now a marina on the canal with horse-drawn barge trips. You can visit Walkley Clogs, by road or towpath or canal barge, to see clogs still being made in the traditional fashion. 20,000 pairs a year are now made, but in its heyday over one million a year were completed. The Automobile and Transport Museum in the town houses the car used by 'James Herriot' in the series 'All Creatures Great and Small'. There is a 1510 packhorse bridge in the town centre. Hostelries abound and it will be hard to continue on the Great English Walk!

TWENTY FIVE

Hebden Bridge - Haworth
(11.0 miles or 17.6 km)

The route out of the town starts by going over Hebden Water by means of the packhorse bridge built in 1510, then going up the opposite cobbled 'road' (signed footpath to Heptonstall). This is a <u>very</u> steep climb to meet a metalled road. Turn right on the road for 100m then go diagonally left, onto a footpath with many steps and more cobbles to reach a second minor road. Turn right for 150m, then left onto a footpath – which immediately splits around a house. Go right, behind the house, and follow the path as it bends right to meet an estate road in the village of Heptonstall.

Stoodley Pike is some 3.5km across the valley south of this point. The Pike is a landmark on the Pennine Way. It was to be built to commemorate the peace of Ghent, but abandoned when Napoleon escaped from Elba, and then completed later after Waterloo. The first monument collapsed in 1854 and was rebuilt at a cost of £812. It is a favourite area of Bernard Ingrams, who was Margaret Thatcher's press secretary when she was Prime Minister.

Turn right on the road (Longfield) to reach a T junction with Hepton Drive, then turn right for 50m, then left onto a flagged path

Heptonstall and Hebden Bridge

Packhorse bridge at Hebden Bridge

to the churchyard railings. Don't enter the churchyard but turn right to follow the railings and pass the quaint weavers' cottages. Just after a right bend turn left up some steps (signed Museum) to reach the churches.

Heptonstall was a handloom weaving centre of some 4000 people, but was transformed when the Rochdale canal was built through the valley and the little hamlet of Hebden Bridge was developed into the town we see today. The town declined and was passed by when the industrial revolution came to the area. In 1847 a terrible storm severely damaged the church of St Thomas à Becket. Instead of repairing the church a new one was built alongside, with the remains of the old 1260 church looking likely to stand forever. The floor of the ruin is paved with old headstones laid face down

and has a rather eerie atmosphere. The church graveyard is reputed to contain 100,000 bodies (although some say it is 10,000). One of the lasting memories of a dark day is church gargoyles—

The name gargoyle comes from the French *gargui,* a medieval dragon which prowled the River Seine, whose horrible image became the symbol of the souls of the condemned turned to stone, or alternatively the devils and the demons of the underworld spared eternal damnation!

The town today has wonderful stone houses and an early 17th century school converted to a museum. The museum contains a display about John Hartley and his followers, the famous Cragg Vale coiners. They were a party of people who 'clipped' official coins and made forged coins from

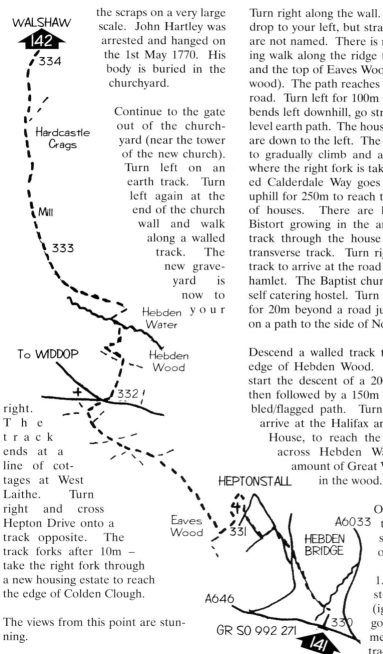

WALSHAW
142
334
Hardcastle Crags
Mill
333
Hebden Water
To WIDDOP
Hebden Wood
332
HEPTONSTALL
Eaves Wood
331
A6033
HEBDEN BRIDGE
A646
GR SO 992 271
141
330

the scraps on a very large scale. John Hartley was arrested and hanged on the 1st May 1770. His body is buried in the churchyard.

Continue to the gate out of the churchyard (near the tower of the new church). Turn left on an earth track. Turn left again at the end of the church wall and walk along a walled track. The new graveyard is now to your

Turn right along the wall. There is a sheer drop to your left, but strangely these crags are not named. There is now an exhilarating walk along the ridge through boulders and the top of Eaves Wood (a natural Oak wood). The path reaches a metalled minor road. Turn left for 100m then, as the road bends left downhill, go straight ahead on a level earth path. The houses of Lumb Bank are down to the left. The path soon begins to gradually climb and a fork is reached where the right fork is taken (the signposted Calderdale Way goes left). Continue uphill for 250m to reach the back of a line of houses. There are large patches of Bistort growing in the area. Follow the track through the house line, to meet a transverse track. Turn right on the earth track to arrive at the road junction at Slack hamlet. The Baptist church here is now a self catering hostel. Turn right on the road for 20m beyond a road junction, then left on a path to the side of No. 30.

Descend a walled track to reach the top edge of Hebden Wood. Turn half-left to start the descent of a 200m zig, which is then followed by a 150m zag down a cobbled/flagged path. Turn left before you arrive at the Halifax and District Scout House, to reach the stepping stones across Hebden Water. A large amount of Great Wood-rush grows in the wood.

On the far side of the stepping stones there are 2 options—

1. Climb up the stoned path (ignoring path going off right) to meet a wide forest track. Turn left on

right. The track ends at a line of cottages at West Laithe. Turn right and cross Hepton Drive onto a track opposite. The track forks after 10m – take the right fork through a new housing estate to reach the edge of Colden Clough.

The views from this point are stunning.

Lumb bridge waterfall

this to reach Gibson Mill OR

2. Turn left along the riverside to follow a path to Gibson Mill.

Gibson Mill was built in 1800 as a water-powered cotton mill, with a 5 horse power wheel. The power source was changed to a steam engine in 1860, but competition meant manufacturing ceased in 1890.

Carry on along the track to the right of the mill. Hardcastle Crags are to the right but little can be seen because of the dense trees. Wall Lettuce grows along the track sides. 0.75km brings the track to a fork, with a permissive path going off left – which is taken along a level terrace above Hebden Water. Just after a path rises up from the footbridge down to the left, turn right up through trees and follow a minor stream. Near the top of the tree line is a small waterfall to the right. There used to be a viewing bridge but this has collapsed. At this point turn left to leave the Scots Pine

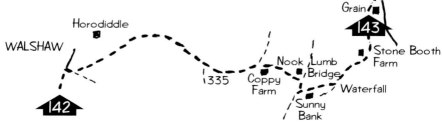

wood over a stile. Follow a right wall for 50m, then head straight across the field to arrive to the right of a row of houses. Go through the gate to the right of a wall (behind a pole weathercock) and go over a stile onto a road at Walshaw hamlet.

Turn right onto an earth road, which is left after 30m to go diagonally left through a gate, onto a path signed Crimsworth Dean. The track is initially walled, with the farmhouse of Horodiddle over to the left. The walls end, but the track carries on to reach another wall and bear right. The wall is now followed towards Shackleton Knoll. The area is full of the calls of curlews and lapwings and you should also see wheatears and red grouse. Follow the wall as it curves around the knoll, until 50m short of a cross wall where the path goes through a left gate. Follow the wall now to your right. As the path reaches the ruin of Coppy Farm the track splits. Go right through a gate and down a walled track. Pass Coppy Farm and reach the ruined Nook Farm. At this point there are numerous paths. Turn right onto a wide access track for 100m, then sharp left down a track to yet another ruin, this time of Sunny Bank Farm.

Continue past the farm to reach Crimsworth Dean and the beautiful waterfall at Lumb Bridge. This is a very good spot to linger. When you have refreshed yourselves, cross the packhorse bridge to continue on the same line – straight uphill to the left of a wall. Cross a small field and go over a stile to the right of Stone Booth farmhouse. This is a little tricky! Turn left

before a barn, then up 5 steps and through a stile into a field. Head straight across the field to a wall on the left, then over a stile, through a gate twixt barn and Grain farmhouse, to arrive on the farm access road. Walk up the 'road' to meet the Old Haworth road.

Turn left on the road and descend to cross the bridge over Grain Water, and then ascend until the tarmac runs out as the access track to Thurrish Farm is reached. Carry on a straight line forward as the track now becomes unsurfaced. This is the old road to Haworth, and a very lonely road it must have been. To the left is Stairs Dyke, with Stairs Edge and Swamp to the right. The highest point is 425m (1395 feet) and goes by the obvious name of Top of Stairs! The 'road' finally begins to descend. Go through a gate and bear right as the route reaches a wall and passes over a water conduit. The route becomes lined with broken walls and reaches another gate where the name changes from Stairs to Bodkin Lane. Leeshaw Reservoir comes into view and Bodkin Farm is passed on the final descent.

Follow the track along the side and dam of the reservoir until it makes a sharp right turn. Go 50m past the turn then (opposite Lee House) turn left up the access track to Westfield Farm. Continue past the farm for 2 fields following a right wall and turn right through a stile. Pass Drop Farm (which is now converted to a café), and carry on to

Map labels:

Bodkin

144

338

Top of Stairs
425m

Stairs Edge

337

Thurrish Farm

336

Grain

143

meet metalled Moor Side Lane. Turn left for 50m, then just past a toilet block fork right to enter Penistone Country Park.

Follow the wide track as it goes to the left of the hill. When the track ends at a car park carry on ahead on a path contouring around the left of the hillside. The path crosses a number of other paths, with directions in Japanese (to man-made Brontë waterfall), and descends to meet a road. Cross the road and descend a walled track. At the bottom of the track turn left onto a flagged way, which is followed to a kissing gate giving access to Haworth churchyard. Walk through the churchyard to the right of the church to enter Haworth village (pronounced Howorth by the locals).

Haworth was an industrial town when the Reverend Patrick Brontë and his wife Maria brought their family here in 1820.

Out of 6 children 4 were destined to become famous – Branwell, Charlotte, Emily and Anne. The town was then a centre for the weaving industry and was very dirty and insanitary. All that changed as the children became famous novelists.

Today the town is known for many things: Its shopping street – being cobbled and very hilly, with all manner of shops selling mementoes. There are also many cafés.

Near the bottom of the hill is the railway station on the privately run Keighley and Worth Valley Railway. The trains run from Oxenhope, via Haworth and Oakworth to join the main line track at Keighley in 25 minutes. Trains run for most of the year.

The most famous film to be made 'starring' the line is 'The Railway Children' in 1970 with Bernard Cribbins, Dinah Sheridan,

Churchyard at Haworth

William Mervyn and Jenny Agutter. Other roles for the line have been in the film 'Yanks' (which was also filmed in Stalybridge), and in 'Poirot'.

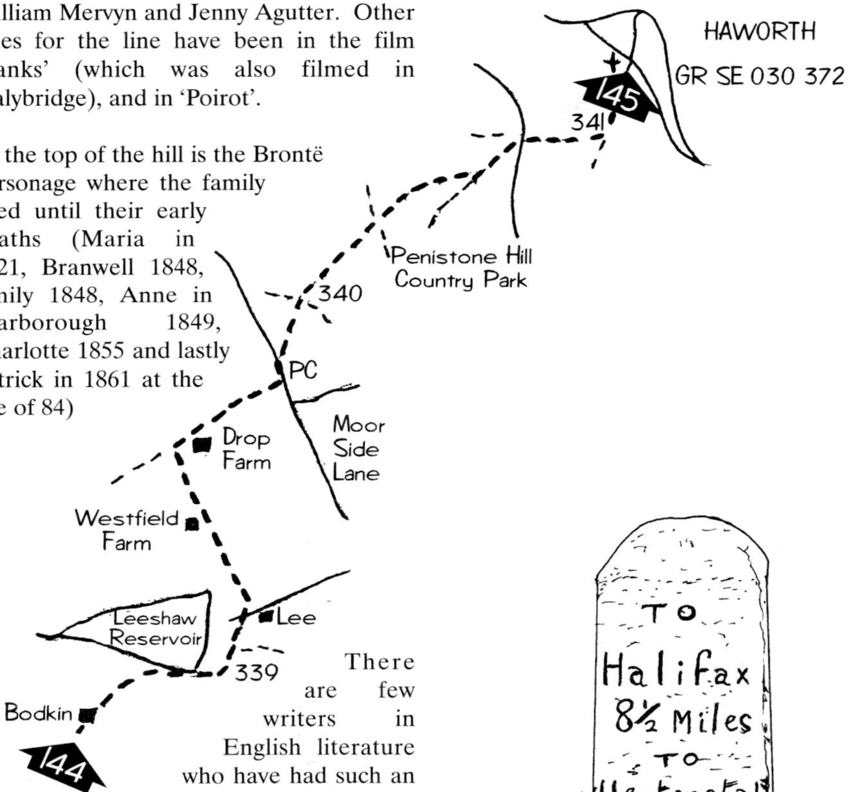

At the top of the hill is the Brontë parsonage where the family lived until their early deaths (Maria in 1821, Branwell 1848, Emily 1848, Anne in Scarborough 1849, Charlotte 1855 and lastly Patrick in 1861 at the age of 84)

HAWORTH
GR SE 030 372

145

341

Penistone Hill Country Park

340

PC

Drop Farm

Moor Side Lane

Westfield Farm

Leeshaw Reservoir

Lee

339

Bodkin

144

There are few writers in English literature who have had such an effect on their readers. There are fewer still whose home and place of writing remains intact.

The parsonage is now a museum restored to resemble the Brontë home.

Charlotte wrote 'The Professor' in 1846, 'Jane Eyre' 1847, 'Shirley' 1849, 'Villette' 1853.

Emily wrote 'Wuthering Heights' 1847.

Anne wrote 'Agnes Grey' 1847, 'Tenant of Wildfell Hall' 1848.

TO
Halifax
8½ Miles
TO
Heptonstal
¼ Mile

Sign at Slack

Mickleden from Mickleden Edge

Dahlias at end of Morton Wood, Scholes

TWENTY SIX
Haworth - Ilkley
(16.5 miles or 26.4 km)

Turn left from the church and then fork right along Changegate. Cross North Street to continue on Changegate (with the Brontë Weaving Shed on the left) and descend for 0.5km to reach Lord Bridge over the River Worth. Follow the road as it turns right and left and starts to climb. 400m after leaving the bridge the road turns sharp right, but at this point go over a stile in the corner to the left and continue uphill in the field, with a wall to the right side. Go through 2 stiles to arrive at the left of a farmhouse. Pass the farm and turn right along a lane to meet a minor road. Turn left on the road for 100m to a cross road, then turn right (note the old building opposite, 'Oakworth Local Board, Water Meter House 1877'). Walk for 100m then turn left along Hillside Avenue. At the end of the avenue take the footpath between Nos. 31 & 33 leading to a stile and into a field. Turn right to follow the left side of a broken wall. Pass through a small gate to the right of a farmhouse and onto an earth road.

Turn right for 100m, then left on a lane for 50m and through a stile. Ignore any right pointing signs and go straight ahead to pass to the left of 2 houses. At the end of the 2nd house turn right down a walled track and follow it as it bends left and right. Keep following the right wall by a very boggy area to climb uphill to an earth access track. Turn right to reach a metalled road (Wide Lane). Turn left on the road for 300m to reach Oakworth Cemetery and

Crematorium. Pass by (although there are some welcome seats in the area) to Slack Lane. Slightly left on the opposite roadside is a stile, over which go diagonally left down to a stile and footbridge over Newsholme Beck. Over another stile follow the right wall and through a stile on the right onto a farm access track. Turn left to a minor road, then left on this to a T junction. Turn right to the village of Newsholme.

Church Farm has a distinctive windmill. Follow the road round as it bears left to pass St John's Church and then forks as it ends. Take the left walled track for 150m, then carry straight on following the right wall. Cross a stile and descend diagonally left into Newsholme Dean. It is a small nicely wooded area. At the

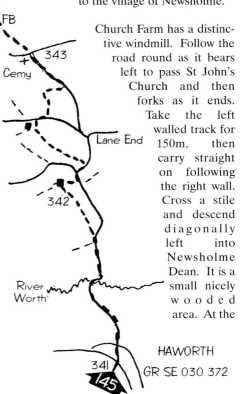

Holme Moss from Upperthong

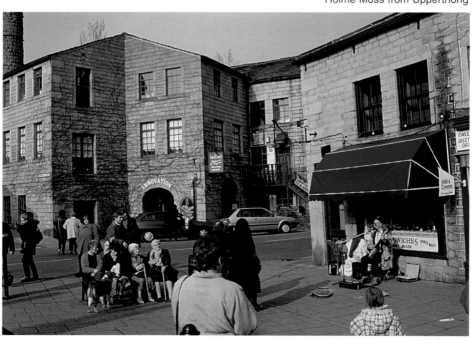

Hebden Bridge

bottom of the dean go through a gate to reach the old clapper bridge (with a more 'modern' one alongside) over Dean Beck. Walk along the access road for 50m only, then go through the gate on the left. Climb the hill between stream to left and house to right, then bear right to meet a bridleway track. Turn left on the track for 20m, then right over a locked gate and climb diagonally left. Follow a right wall for 50m then go straight uphill between the wall and a depression to the left, on the line of a 'removed' wall, to reach a stile onto Todley Hall Road.

Turn left on the road for 50m, then right over a stile. Follow a left wall through a number of fields and stiles on an obvious route. This area is the haunt of fieldfares in winter and spring. The path leads to a minor road.

The next kilometre is, in 1997, messy for route finding. Hopefully North Yorks County Council will address the problems.

Turn left on the road for 150m to cross into North Yorkshire (but don't worry, the GEW will visit West Yorks again on the way to Ilkley before finally entering North Yorks). An old road sign proclaims entry into the county. A further 50m brings you to a gate on the right side (locked). Climb the gate and cross the field at right angles to the road to reach a 2nd barred gate. Over this gate the remains of Pole Stoop long barrow, an ancient burial ground, are to the right. Bear half-left to the left of the barrow and cross a large field to arrive at 2 gates in a fence line. Go through the left gate and again half-left downhill to arrive at the earth road called America Lane. Then, depending on whether you are on the correct path line or not, turn left for 100m to a

Looking back to Haworth

147

FB

Lumb Clough

346

America Farm

Aden Farm

A d e n
F a r m .
The diffi-
cult path
area has now
been passed.

America Lane

345

Pole Stoop

County Boundary

Todley Hall Road

344

Newsholme Dean

146

NEWSHOLME

gate opposite America Farm. Go through the gate and follow a left wall down to the farm. Pass through another fence line and go to the right of the farmhouse (barn to right). Enter the farm 'back garden' and climb down a stileless sunken wall to the right into a lower field. Follow the left side wall until it ends, then turn half-left to reach the right side of

Turn left to go in front of the farmhouse, go through a gate, then turn half-right to pass through a second gate and turn right to end up on the left side of a stream. After 50m the path changes to the right stream side and a left wall is followed down to a clapper bridge. Sweet Cicely can be found along the path. Cross the bridge and climb the hill, bearing right around a wall. Upon reaching a 2nd cross wall, don't cross but turn left to climb the field and go over a stile into a farmyard. Cross concrete and go over a stile into a field. Follow the left wall and find a gate 50m to the right of

the far left corner. Descend into Lumb Clough and down to Lumb Clough Beck. There are carpets of Ramsons (Wild Garlic) and Wood-sorrel.

Cross the beck and turn right on a path. Opposite-leaved Golden-saxifrage, Hard-fern, Bluebells, and many more species are all found here in abundance – a very beautiful valley. Half a kilometre brings you to a footbridge, which is crossed to follow the beck on its right bank. The lower reaches of the valley are planted with Rhododendron, Daffodils and Holly species from the days when this was the private Sutton Hall estate. Keep on the right bank and ignore left bridges, then cross a footbridge on the direct line ahead to enter an unmade estate road. Pass through the archway and lodges of the long demolished Sutton Hall. The hall was built by local mill owners, who lived there from 1884 to 1934. When you reach West Lane turn right for 10m then left onto High Street in Sutton-in-Craven.

At the first bend turn left into North Road and continue straight ahead into Hazel Grove, at the end of which cross a footbridge over Holme Beck. Turn right into a narrow passage twixt gardens and beck to reach Holme Lane. Turn left to meet the houses of Cross Hills. Continue on the lane to reach the A6068 Colne Road. Turn right , then left at a fork onto Station Road. Carry on to cross the railway bridge (the Kildwick and Cross Hills station is long since gone) and almost reach the roundabout of the A629 road. 40m short of the roundabout turn left onto a footpath going under the bypass road, to reach the River Aire (the 2nd of the SUNWAC river series), and then turn left to cross the 1305 (widened in 1780) bridge over the river and into Kildwick.

The name Kildwick probably means '*a dwelling place by the spring of water*'. The Domesday survey of 1086 records a church, and it is thought that the church of St Andrew could well date back to the late 9th century. Further north there are many records of Scots' invasions, and it is known that they penetrated this far south in the 12th century. The present church is one of the largest in Yorkshire. Inside is the de Stiverton monument dated at 1307. Sir Robert de Stiverton was knighted by Edward I, for services against the Scots.

Kildwick Hall dates from 1673, and was the home of the Currer family for many years. There is a school of thought that Charlotte Brontë knew the house and was the reason why she chose her *nom-de-plume* of Currer.

Just north of the bridge turn right onto the broad path alongside the River Aire until a cattle grid is reached (at a place called Kildwick Ings). The path goes over a stile and bears left along a Hawthorn/wire hedge. The hedge ends at an embankment, but carry on the same direction and skirt left of a small ox-bow pond (the river has changed course a number of times over the years and this is the remains of an old course). Go over a stile and turn half-left, aiming to cross the field to a solitary Oak tree 70m right of the left field corner. A stile brings a right wall, which bends and changes to a Hawthorn hedge. The tower on Hawk Cliff is very clear on the south side of the valley. At the field end go left of a line of trees, but still on the same line and head back towards the river. Keep along the riverbank, pass a stand of Willow trees and take stiles through 2 stone walls. Leave the river by heading half-left across a field

Lumb Clough Beck

to reach the A6034 Silsden Road at a point half way between the left wall and the river. The centre of Silsden is 1.3km to the left.

Go slightly left on the road, then right to a path and over an old packhorse bridge. Cross the field partly left to a stile onto an embankment, which is crossed and followed by a field on the same line to reach a solid stone stile. Follow the left fence (and ignore stile on right), go through a stile and turn half-right through a gap in a wall. A half-left direction is now taken to a gate at the field end, soon followed by another stile, then a left fence/wall is followed through a large field to far stile. Turn half-left in the field, through a gate and a small field to a stile in the last field before Howden House. Cross a field with the converted house over to the right side. Go through a stile at the far left of the house, turning right in a field to a stile onto a metalled minor road.

Turn left on the road, pass a junction left,

then after a further 100m turn right through a gate (if locked then alternatively you can continue along the road to the canal, then right along the towpath to reach*). The wall to the right is soon left and the path crosses a ford over Holden Beck. Bear half-left, to follow a right fence and reach the Leeds to Liverpool canal. The canal opened for the first through, Leeds to Liverpool boats, on the 23rd October 1816. This is a broad canal capable of carrying much larger boats than the Huddersfield Narrow. It is now an extremely popular holiday canal.

*Cross a swing bridge and go along the access track to Howden Park Farm, through the yard and reach a minor road. Turn right for a stiff road climb. When the road bends sharp right there is a welcome seat with views over the Aire Valley to the south. Leave the road here through a gate/stile onto a farm access track. When the track swings left down to a house carry straight on. The path soon reaches the trees of Holden Beck Wood on the left. Climb up to a wall but don't pass through the gate. Continue along the wall side above the wood. When the sound of water is heard

A613   + KILDWICK   A6068   A629   349   148   River Calder   348   CROSS HILLS   A6068   Holme Beck   347   SUTTON-IN-CRAVEN   147   148   349   River Calder   350   To SILSDEN   A6034   149   River Calder

take the path going left down steps to reach the double Holden Beck waterfalls. This is a beautiful area full of Moschatel, Ramsons, Opposite-leaved Golden-saxifrage, Wood-sorrel, Violets and a variety of Ferns.

Retrace the route back up the steps to the higher path and turn left. Cross a tributary and pass through both Western and European Gorse. Suddenly a sewer pipe crosses the valley at a high level! Cross a footbridge over another waterfall and climb the field to the right of the pipe. As a wall is neared, bear right to keep the wall to the left. Go through a gate in the top corner and follow the left wall to Ghyll Grange Farm. At the 1st barn go left through a gate and follow the farm road around the buildings to another gate. Turn right at a track crossroads and follow signs as the route goes into the farmyard and then in front of the farmhouse. Follow

the 'road' left of a large house, bearing right around the house, through a gate and follow the track to the left of a wall. Keep on the track when the wall ends and soon a left wall starts. Walk over a cattle grid (one of many) and leave the track to follow the left wall for 150m, then turn left through a stile at a wall junction.

Follow the left wall uphill and through a gate, around a large boulder, to enter the yard of Doubler Stones Farm and out on a farm road. Cross a transverse track (with bungalow to left) and head straight across the moor passing 2 water chambers. The path now reaches the Doubler Stones. These are formed of hard grit on sandstone. The western stone has several cup mark carvings, and the eastern one has 2

Howden Beck Waterfall 150

Wood

Howden Park Farm

352

149

351

Howden House

Howden Beck

Leeds-Liverpool Canal

Doubler Stones

cups. The whole area is called Rombalds Moor, with individual names for smaller areas. This particular area is Addingham High Moor. Head due north following a distinct path which climbs past grouse butts, to a stile in a wall at the 'summit' of Black Hill. The height is 381m. 100m beyond the wall the ridge top is reached, with Addingham village far below. Turn right along the ridge. There are a number of stiles and walls to cross, with a number of named outcrops below the ridge. The ridge outcrops are nowhere near as fine as Derwent Edge, but nonetheless are very nice.

The ridge becomes less impressive as Ilkley town grows nearer.

Stile on Black Hill

Sparse Larch trees have been planted in some places. The obvious path is followed along the ridge until a reservoir is finally sighted, just before which is the railed Swastika Stone. The moor has the most cup and ring stones to be found in the whole of the country, carved between 2800 and 500BC. The Swastika mark is of a later date than the other C and R marks and is

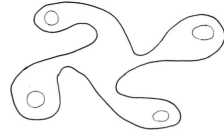

Swastika Stone

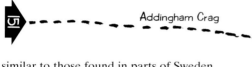

Addingham Crag

355

Swastika Stone

similar to those found in parts of Sweden.

Past the stone a wood and wall join from the left. Keep to the right of the wall and go over a substantial footbridge over Black Beck to reach the reservoir. A line of houses is reached. The moor to the right is now Ilkley Moor. Everyone must now remove

their hats to faithfully render—

1. Wheer wor ta bahn when ah saw thee

On Ilkla Moor baht 'at? (Chorus)

Bridge on Ilkley Moor

repeat main line twice again followed by chorus 3 times.

2. *Tha's bin a-courtin' Mary Jane*
3. *Tha's bin to get the deeath o'cowd*
4. *Then we shall ha' to bury thee*
5. *Then t'wurms 'll coom, an' ate thee oop*
6. *Then t'ducks 'll coom an' ate oop t'wurms*
7. *Then we shall go an' ate oop t'ducks*
8. *Then we shall all 'ave etten thee*
9. *That's wheer we get us oahn back*

Some say the song was composed by a visiting Halifax choir, whilst others claim it was written by a Victorian Lincolnshire clergyman.

Carry on the route, leaving the houses behind and cross a bridge to arrive at a metalled road. Turn left on the road for 150m, then turn right onto a path (opposite a seat and a 'No Off Road Driving' sign). Walk over a covered reservoir to join an unmade road and cross a ford (water only runs after heavy rain). Carry on the road to reach White Wells. The wells were first recorded in the 14th century, but must have been known long before that date. The nat-

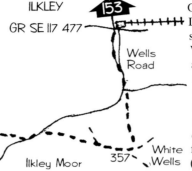

White Wells

Calder Valley

Lumb Clough Beck

The Shawl, Leyburn

ural water can be sampled in the café and anyone can have a FREE bath in the bath-house...by appointment only. A plaque records that the bath house, built by Squire Middleton in the 18th century for the people of Ilkley, was restored in 1972/4. The café is open if the Union Flag is flying from the masthead.

Just past the house turn left and descend steps to a path passing a paddling pool, to reach Crossbeck Road and descend Wells Road to Ilkley town centre.

The rail line from Leeds (opened in 1865) now terminates at Ilkley, but originally ran west to serve Addingham, Bolton Abbey, Embsay and on to Skipton. The stretch from Embsay to Skipton now operates as a restored private line. The Manor House is built on the site of an old Roman camp of AD79. The Roman name for the camp was Olicana. There are 3 ancient crosses in the parish church of All Saints, variously dated to Roman, Celtic, Runic or Saxon periods!

Route to Blubberhouses

Reflections in River Ure

TWENTY SEVEN
Ilkley - Pateley Bridge
(18.5 miles or 29.6 km)

Leave Ilkley by walking down Brook Street. Cross the River Wharfe bridge (built 1904). This is the 3rd river crossed in the SUNWAC series. Just over the bridge turn right down to the riverside and follow a path all the way to Denton Road. Turn right along the road verge to pass the suspension bridge. In a further 500m the Nell Bank complex is reached and 150m beyond this is a stile on the left. Over the stile head diagonally right to cross the field to a stile in the far corner. Cross the next field to exit onto Carter's Lane. Walk down the drive opposite, over Bow Beck bridge and reach Beckfoot Farm. Go through the centre of the farm buildings and pass to the right of the farmhouse. A stile

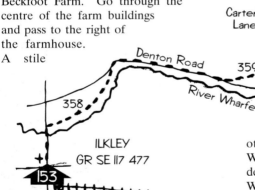

takes the path onto an embankment to the left of a shippon. Cross a stile and a small field, then turn right along the fenced off West Park Wood (with Bluebells, Ramsons, Ground Ivy and Greater Stitchwort). The wood eventually ends and the fence keeps on to join a minor road. Turn left on the road to the centre of Denton village.

In the village centre is the carved stone known as *'The Powder Puff'*. Turn right.

There is a rare VR postbox with letter flap on the right. Letter boxes were introduced into Great Britain by Anthony Trollope, a Post Office clerk (later surveyor), in 1852. Trollope went on to become a successful author with books such as *The Barchester Chronicles*.

The road forks here and the left fork is taken along Smithy Lane. A farm is passed after 300m. Just after this point are 2 gates and then a stile on the left. Cross the stile and head up the field at right angles, keeping to the left of a small stream. At the top of the field are 4 Alder trees alongside a stile, on the other side of which is a stream (with Watercress). Walk up the field aiming for a depression in the ridge, which is just left of Willow Hill Farm – following a right wall at first, then a left wall to pass left of the farmhouse. As the ridge is topped Yarnett House Farm appears ahead. Go straight on to a gate (150m southwest of the farmhouse). Through the gate go half-left across a field to the corner of a fence and broken wall. Turn left round the wall for 50m to a fence stile, then half-right across the next field aiming for a stile (to the left of a gate) in the wall on the horizon. Over this stile aim for the far left corner of the next field, go through a gate and turn left along a short wall to reach an access track from Moorside Farm.

Turn right on the stony track for 250m, go over a cattle grid and turn r i g h t through a gate. Cross 2 fields and

155

361

360
154

● Yarnett House Farm

■Willow Hill Farm

T

+

DENTON

2 gates, then turn left for 100m to a cross wall, go through the gate and turn right along the wall to

reach the drive of Dunkirk Farm. Turn left along the drive to reach the gate of the farm garden. Do not hesitate at this point, enter the garden and walk up to the front door of the farmhouse – then turn right to exit through a gate into a field. It is amazing how a glorious garden can be created from nothing on open moorland. Through the gate turn left and follow the wall through a gate into another field, which is crossed on the same line to a stile giving access to the open Denton Moor. There is no obvious path across the moor, but the route takes the same line as that from the farm. It may be advisable to take a compass bearing of 20 degrees. If route finding is correct then a track is met coming from the left, soon followed by a wall – if not then turn right along the wall to reach the high point of Ellarcarr Pike.

Powder Puff at Denton

On the horizon to the east is a vast collection of radar domes (a gaggle, pride, flock or radomery?). Take a stile over the wall. To the left is the entrance drive to Ellercarr House (some trouble with spelling in this area!), but turn right to follow the stone driveway downhill. Bear left and right as High Wood is reached. 300m brings the buildings of Sourby Farm on the right. Opposite the 1st building is

Ellercarr

Wall

Ellarcarr Pike

363

Field Limit

Dunkirk

362

155

part of Beecroft Moor plantation. Take care – trees soon start on the right and after a further 300m a faint path appears both left and right. Turn left onto a path which soon becomes more obvious as it goes through dense trees to reach a footbridge over Thackray Beck. Enter the ruins of Ridge Bottom House and then head up a green lane behind the old house. When the lane peters out cross a stile, follow the right fence for 50m until it bends right, then strike out ahead across the field to a broken wall and stile behind a single Oak tree. Keep on the same line

Victorian post box at Denton

a stile on the left. A left wall is followed through the 1st and 2nd fields. Fewston Reservoir is over to the right with the radar domes beyond. Pass over 2 more stiles which take the path to the right of Hillside Farm. In the field beyond the farm head for a stile 50m right of the far left bottom corner. Over this follow the left hedge, then another stile to a ruined farm. Turn right along the farm access track (with a wall to right), then through a gate onto a wide transverse track, which is crossed to head across a field on the same line. Pass through a gap and turn half-right, over another stile and follow a wall to pass Grange Cottage on the left. After a few metres pass through a gate onto the cottage access drive which soon meets Rues Lane.

Cross the lane, through a gate, onto the opposite track. The trees to the left are

Beech trees along River Washburn

Canoeists on the River Washburn

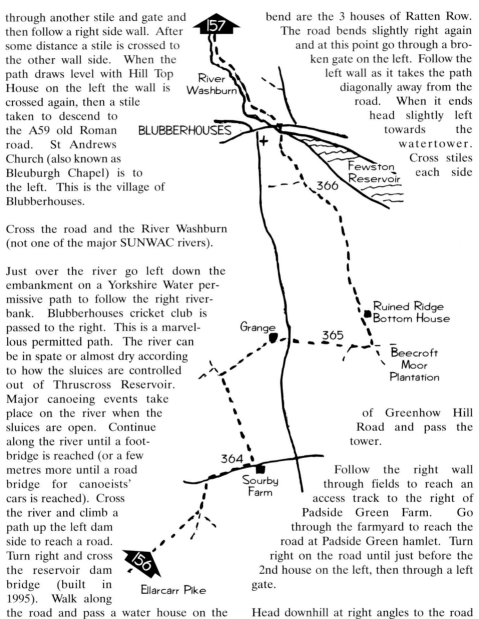

through another stile and gate and then follow a right side wall. After some distance a stile is crossed to the other wall side. When the path draws level with Hill Top House on the left the wall is crossed again, then a stile taken to descend to the A59 old Roman road. St Andrews Church (also known as Bleuburgh Chapel) is to the left. This is the village of Blubberhouses.

Cross the road and the River Washburn (not one of the major SUNWAC rivers).

Just over the river go left down the embankment on a Yorkshire Water permissive path to follow the right riverbank. Blubberhouses cricket club is passed to the right. This is a marvellous permitted path. The river can be in spate or almost dry according to how the sluices are controlled out of Thruscross Reservoir. Major canoeing events take place on the river when the sluices are open. Continue along the river until a footbridge is reached (or a few metres more until a road bridge for canoeists' cars is reached). Cross the river and climb a path up the left dam side to reach a road. Turn right and cross the reservoir dam bridge (built in 1995). Walk along the road and pass a water house on the right, then continue along the quiet road which climbs past Gate Inn Cottage just before the road bears right. Beyond this

bend are the 3 houses of Ratten Row. The road bends slightly right again and at this point go through a broken gate on the left. Follow the left wall as it takes the path diagonally away from the road. When it ends head slightly left towards the watertower. Cross stiles each side

of Greenhow Hill Road and pass the tower.

Follow the right wall through fields to reach an access track to the right of Padside Green Farm. Go through the farmyard to reach the road at Padside Green hamlet. Turn right on the road until just before the 2nd house on the left, then through a left gate.

Head downhill at right angles to the road following a 'bendy' left wall to reach Padside Beck. At the beck itself go through the left wall to find a small footbridge and wall stile beyond (with, in 1997, a high barbed wire fence beyond). Cross a field half-left and then follow the left fence up to a barn. The route now becomes a little tricky! Go to the right of the barn, follow a left wall, go through a gate, descend to a small stone bridge near White House Farm, go through a gate and turn immediately left through a 2nd gate. Go half-right and through a 3rd gate, then follow the field uphill with wall/fence to *left*. At the end of the 1st field the stile is 20m from the left corner. Climb the next field aiming for the gate to the right of Banger House farmhouse. Cross a stile to the left of a gate and go round to the right of the farm following the left wall. Pass through a gate and cross an open field and over a stile. Follow a left wall for 50m then cross a stone bridge over Black Sike. Turn half-left and head straight for Grange House. Go through a gate and turn right on the farm access road to reach the junction with Dike Lane.

Turn left for 50m, then leave the lane by turning right over a stile opposite Dyke Lane Head Farm. Follow the right wall, over a stile and head straight across the next field on same line to a stile in the opposite wall. Cross the next field aiming directly for a house at Heyshaw hamlet. Go left of the house to reach a minor road. Turn right on the road to reach a 'road' junction, where a left turn is taken on an access road signed Guise Cliff. Pass Heyshaw Cottage on the left and bear right with the access road as it

climbs. Nidderdale valley is now clear to the east, with the Yorkshire plain beyond. Hill Top Farm is soon passed at 276m. Go through a gate to follow a private road, passing abandoned quarries, to arrive at High Hood Gap Farm – which blocks the direct way ahead. 50m short of the farm go through a gate on the right and then follow a left wall to pass the farm. Go through a gate into an open field, heading slightly right to go to the *right* side of a wall. Next go over a stile to enter open moorland.

Carry on the same line, crossing another path, to climb up Guise Cliff. Walk along the ridge top with its collection of spectacular rocks (and a TV repeater station to the left). Pateley Bridge is now clear below, with Gouthwaite Reservoir beyond. Continue along this spectacular permissive path until a stile is reached, when the view is curtailed by a wall to the right. Cross a stile and reach Yorke's Folly – which must have provided work for someone. Continue on the path past the folly and descend to Nought Bank Road at a road bend. Cross the road to go half-right downhill on an obvious path into Skrikes Wood. The path through the wood was once cobbled. Leave the wood and continue descending across a field to reach Nought Bank Road again. Turn left for 100m then, at a road bend, go through a gate and turn left down many steps and cross a field to enter Skrikes Wood again. This is an exquisite walk along a streamside through a private nature reserve. Watch out for the elusive dipper. All good things have to come to an end and all too soon a footbridge is crossed taking the path to a minor road.

Turn right along the walled road, with Herb Robert growing in the walls. On the left after 250m is the drive to White Wood Farm. Turn onto the drive for 5m, then sharp right onto a wide path which passes through a Rhododendron plantation to reach a small pond (filled with Bulrushes and Marsh-marigolds). At the pool end go

over a footbridge and left to a kissing gate. Turn right along the wallside and climb 24 steps. At the ridge top go through a stile then downhill again to the far right field corner and onto a minor road. Turn left for 50m, cross a stream and turn right into a field. Head diagonally left climbing up to a stile, near a lamppost on the B6265

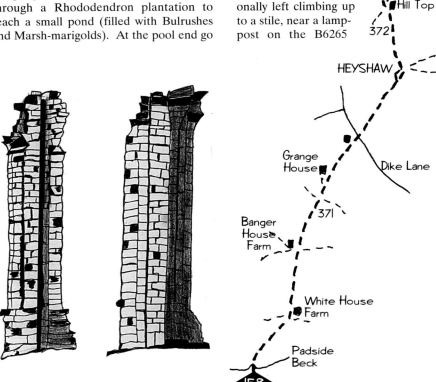

Nought Bank Road

159

Yorke's Folly 374

Guise Cliff

373

High Head Gap Farm

Hill Top

372

HEYSHAW

Grange House

Dike Lane

371

Banger House Farm

White House Farm

Padside Beck

158

Yorke's Folly

road. Turn right on the road for the short walk down to the 18th century triple arched bridge over the River Nidd (the N of SUNWAC) and into the town.

Pateley Bridge was known as *Patleia* in the 12th century (*a path through the glade*). There used to be several water powered flax mills in the town. A rail line was built from Harrogate in 1860/2 to Pateley (closed 1964), and there was even a separate line up the dale built in 1904 – but this closed in 1936. Upper Nidderdale is now 'an Area of Outstanding Natural Beauty'. St Mary's medieval church was abandoned in 1827, and there is a museum of Nidderdale in the town.

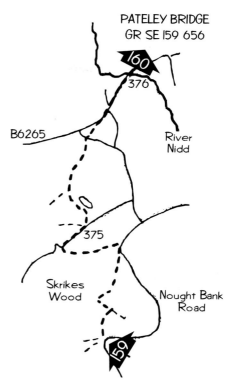

PATELEY BRIDGE
GR SE 159 656

160

376

B6265

River
Nidd

375

Skrikes
Wood

Nought Bank
Road

159

Glasshouses from Guise Cliff

TWENTY EIGHT
Pateley Bridge - Masham
(17.8 miles or 28.5 km)

Leave the town by walking up High Street. Bear right on Ripon Road for 200m, then go left up 11 steps (signed

PATELEY BRIDGE
GR SE 159 656

Panoramic Walk). After a few metres on the left is an old stone with a very worn inscription 'The way to Church'. The steep tarmaced track is followed to pass a cemetery on the left. Snowberry, Garlic Mustard, Nipplewort, Violets and Hairy Bitter-cress line the track. There is a viewing area at one point. The houses of Knott hamlet are reached, beyond which the tarmac road swings right. Carry on forward on a stony track which soon becomes a walled bridle-way. There are excellent views across the valley to Guise Cliff

Pateley Bridge from Ripley Bank

and Yorke's Folly.

The path reaches a road. Turn left to Blazefield, but turn off the road at the first houses to pass a line of very nice terraced houses and some bungalows, to reach a minor road. Turn right for 150m, then left at the 2nd track. Go through a gate and round to the left of a garage, then through a gate to follow a left wall, through stiles and fields to arrive at Raikes hamlet. Cross a minor road and go through the opposite stile (to left of an entry track) and into a narrow path leading to open fields. Follow a right wall. Glasshouses village is down to the right. Just before the end of the 3rd field go over a stile on the right and head for the left side of Kiln Farm. Pass through 2 gates between house and barn and follow a left wall through 2 fields to a track. Turn left for 20m, then left again on a walled track (with Cragg Hall to the right). Barren Strawberry lines the track which climbs up to White Houses (a collection of a few houses). Carry on the track to a 'cross road'. Turn 90 degrees right downhill and pass Faraway House on the left. Bear left and then, as the track bears right, carry straight on through 2 gates aiming for a wood on the horizon. Follow a left wall/fence down to Fell Beck.

As the beck is reached bear 50m away from the left fence corner, then through a fence to cross the beck as best you can. (The beck should be crossable at all times, but if in the middle of winter after a lot of rain, then you could alternatively carry on north from White Houses to Grove Cottage and east along the signed Nidderdale Way, over a beck bridge, and then turn south along a path to rejoin the GEW at *). Follow a broken wall to the left up through the trees and the vague path soon picks up a track between walls. A track coming from the right is met. At this point carry on uphill between walls (do not take the path signed left*). A farm is soon reached. Go over a stile and continue on the farm drive, which is followed as it goes up and swings left and right. Go through a gate and bear right towards the National Trust owned Druids Cave Farm, but before reaching the farm pass a barn on the left – and go through the gate on the left 50m beyond the barn. Turn behind the barn and through rocks, keeping approximately on the same contour, to follow a left wall around the base of Brimham Rocks. The rock outcrops and Brimham Moor beyond are now NT property. Follow the wall and as a farm (High North Pasture) is passed over to the left, go through a stile to continue the same line on its access drive.

Leave the drive after 20m through the 2nd gate on the left. Follow a left wall through a field to a gate, then head across the next field and 2 gates to North Pasture (a farm converted into dwellings). Pass between converted barns and once beyond them turn left to a gate on the left, turning right immediately. Don't gain height but head for a stile in a depression at the end of the 1st field. Cross the next field to a cross wall and turn right along it to climb up between 2 walls. 2 gates are reached to the left of a walled 'garden' of a farmhouse. Go through the right gate onto a farm access track, which is followed to reach a minor road.

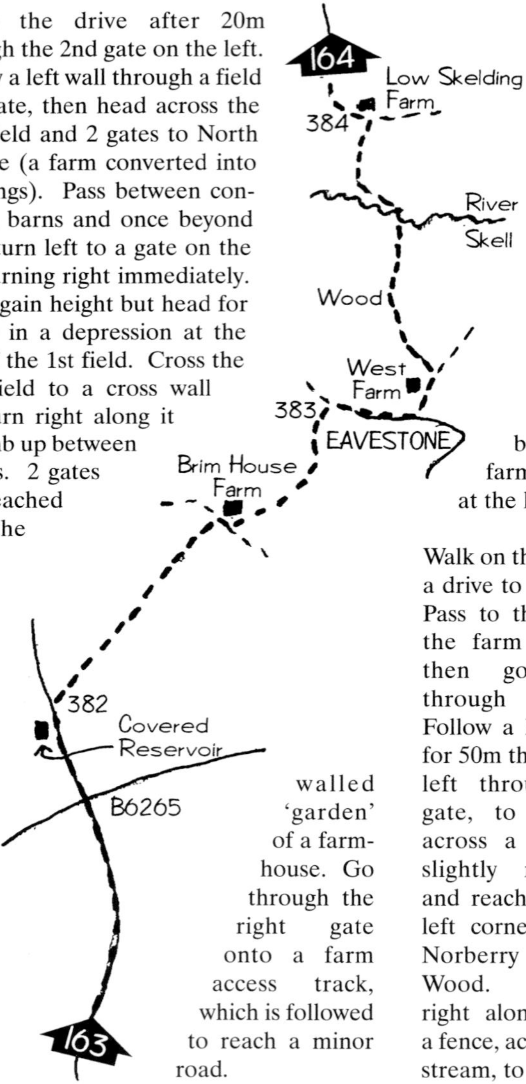

right off the drive to cross the field to a gate. Beyond the gate is an obvious track, which follows a right fence, through many fields to reach Brim House Farm. Just before the farmhouse turn right onto a farm drive for 50m, then left over a stile and follow the left wall to meet several gates. Go through the first gate, then turn left and go through a second (i.e. turn half-left). Head downhill to the left of a fence line. Follow the fence as it bends right and becomes first a farm track and then a metalled road, at the hamlet of Eavestone.

Walk on the road for 200m then turn left on a drive to West Farm. Pass to the right of the farm complex, then go ahead through a gate. Follow a left wall for 50m then turn left through a gate, to head across a field slightly right and reach the left corner of Norberry Hill Wood. Turn right alongside a fence, across a stream, to reach

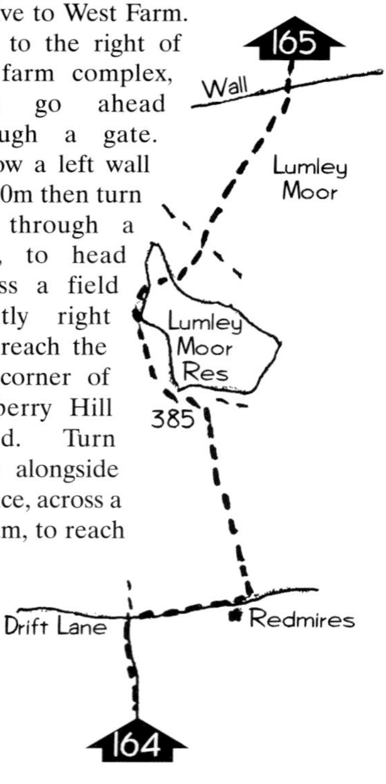

Turn left along the road for 1km to reach its junction with the B6265. Cross this road and along the farm access drive opposite (signed Smaden Head Farm). Pass over a cattle grid and part way into the 2nd field there is a small covered reservoir on the left. At this point turn

Map labels: 164, Low Skelding Farm, 384, River Skell, Wood, West Farm, 383, EAVESTONE, Brim House Farm, 382, Covered Reservoir, B6265, 163, 165, Wall, Lumley Moor, Lumley Moor Res, 385, Drift Lane, Redmires, 164

the end of the wood at a solitary Oak tree. Turn slightly left to cross the next field to a stile, then head straight downhill to concrete stepping stones over the infant River Skell.. Go slightly left through a gate and follow the river for 100m, then strike uphill between 2 large rock outcrops. Keep to the right of a tributary stream as the path climbs and cross a field to a gate, to the right of Low Skelding Farm buildings. Go through the gate and pass in front of the farmhouse. Follow the farm road as it bends right and becomes an adopted tarmac road. After 600m the road meets the larger Drift Lane.

and Lumley Moor Reservoir has been reached. Turn left along the wall and cross a bridge over the Holborn Beck feeder. A causeway is crossed, at the end of which the route goes over a stile straight ahead under a large Scots Pine tree (and leaves the reservoir). Turn half-left and aim for a point about 300m to the right of New Plantation Wood as Lumley Moor is crossed. A broken wall and fence are crossed en route. The 'point' is reached 50m left of the junction of 2 walls. Cross into a walled track, cross this into the next field and continue to the right of a wall. This side of the track is called Galphay Moor. Follow the wall for one and a half fields, then go over a stile on the left to a stile 50m left of a lone barn. Cross the next field and make for the right of a small wood. A left fence/hedge is followed for some distance until a solid stone stile is reached. Turn right and pass through a 100m stretch of Gorse, then left on a farm track to a minor road. Turn right on the road.

Turn right on Drift Lane for 350m, until just past Redmires House, where the road is left through a gate on the left. Head off following a right hedge until it ends, then strike across open fields (with a stone marker) to the wood ahead. Cross a stile

Laverton hamlet is just to the north, but bypassed. Follow the road until it bends right and at this point take the path going off left. Follow a right fence. 50m into a second field turn sharp right and head for a walled track to Missies. The access track from Missies is tarmaced and is followed all the way to cross the bridge over the River Laver. Over the bridge turn right for a few metres, then turn half-left to find a stile onto a minor road. Turn right on the road for 30m then left over a stile and follow the right hedge. Where the hedge ends strike out up the field on the same line. Keep at least 150m away from the road (on the right) and carry on through 5 stiles to arrive at a very minor road. Turn right for 40m to a 'main' road, with a cemetery opposite. Turn left on the road for a walk into Kirkby

Malzeard (pronounced Kirby Malzed). Lesser Periwinkle and Honesty line the road.

The village name indicates Danish origin (*Kirkby*), with Norman influence (*Mal-assart – a poor clearing*). Roger de Mowbray built a castle here about 1080, but it was demolished about 1113. In the village centre is a cross marking the granting of a Market Charter to de Mowbray, by Edward 1, in 1307. The market flourished until 1816, and then lapsed. Pass the cross and walk along the Grewelthorpe road to the church of St Andrew, which was built in 1150 (on the site of an earlier 10th century church). The church records date from 1563, with a list of vicars from 1337. In the graveyard is a tombstone recording the death of George Wharton in 1842 aged 112.

Continue for a short distance on the road to the bridge over Kex Beck. Just as the bridge wall ends on the right enter the wood and climb sharply for 50m to a metal gate giving access to a field. Cross the field

to a tarmac drive and continue across this on the same line, to reach a fence corner. Follow the fence and skirt around the garden of Mowbray View House. The left fence is then followed through a number of fields and stiles until the path enters a field containing a farm over to the right (Newholme Farm). Cross this field and go through one more gate, then turn half-right

across the next field. Go through a stile in the far hedge 50m left of a road. Keep more or less on this line (to the left of a line of houses), to pass through a large number of small fields, until finally

Grewelthorpe village green cross

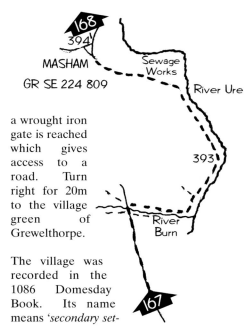

MASHAM

GR SE 224 809

a wrought iron gate is reached which gives access to a road. Turn right for 20m to the village green of Grewelthorpe.

The village was recorded in the 1086 Domesday Book. Its name means *'secondary set-*

tlement' (of Kirkby Malzeard). Turn left at the green (with its Holy cross) to carry on along the road to the north. The road is signed 'Ilton'. Pass 2 road junctions and start climbing Nutwith Lane. 50m past the entrance to 'The Elms' turn right through a stile to the left of an access drive. Turn half-left and aim for the top right hand field corner. Go over a fence to cross the next field on the same line. In the 3rd field climb and bear right. A trig point (215m) comes into view on the right. Head for the hedge north of the trig point and go through a stile. Turn right for 50m, then half-left to descend to a gate giving access to the wood of Horse Pasture Hill. There are a lot of paths in the wood, by kind permission of the Earl of Swinton. Head up the wooded hill to reach the top of a ridge. Go straight across the ridge path and descend to a forest road junction. Turn left on the forest road for 200m, then right on a path through

River Ure

the trees for another 200m, to meet another forest road. This whole area is the old Nutwith Common. Cross this 'road' and descend to yet another forest road as the wood ends. Turn right for 20m onto the road to Masham (Thorpe Road).

Cross the road and turn left on the opposite verge, which soon becomes a wide green bridleway running parallel to the tarmac road. The path runs through Gorse bushes. When the terrain becomes more open follow the right fence line. Masham can now be seen ahead. Join the road again at a bend and walk along it to Low Burn bridge over the River Burn. Silverweed lines the road.

Turn right over the bridge on a path following the River Burn. The path is lined with masses of aniseed smelling Sweet Cicely (a plant not found in the south of England). Follow the river to its confluence with the broad River Ure (the 5th in the SUNWAC series). Turn left along the river bank until the sewage works is reached. The path swings left to join the treatment works road. Turn left on this road, which soon becomes tarmaced and follow it to Masham village, where the village square is soon reached.

The name is pronounced Mass'm. In the 12th century the de Mowbray's, based in Kirkby Malzeard, owned 'Mashamshire'. St Mary's church was established in Saxon times and mentioned in the 1086 Domesday Book. Its tower is Norman based with a 15th century spire and outside the door is the shaft of a 9th century Anglo-Saxon cross with fine figure carvings. The village was an important sheep trading centre in medieval days. Masham today is home to 2 breweries – the Black Sheep and Theakston's ('Old Peculiar'). There is a brewery visitor centre, pottery and a glass works to visit if you have time.

Wild Strawberry *(Fragaria vesca)*

TWENTY NINE
Masham - Leyburn
(16.4 miles or 26.2 km)

Leave the town along the road to the north to a road junction. Pass Bank Villa and turn left on an unnamed street. Bear right behind a row of houses and go alongside the Black Sheep Brewery. Walk along a terraced path on a ridge. Leave the houses and start crossing fields on an unmarked path. Maintain height above the river and keep left of a fence line. The route is not clear, but the fence peters out and then a left fence is followed along another ridge. When a house is seen, head to its left side to cross the access drive and enter Mar Field nature reserve. This is an area of old sand and gravel pits, worked out in 1989 and now managed by Redland Aggregates. There is a right of way through the area, originally through the centre (left of the lakes), then diverted to the right of the lakes, then back to the centre again! The best route seems to be to go ahead for 100m, then bear right just past the old weighbridge. A bird hide has been provided for viewing over the flooded pits (tufted duck, canada geese, coot, swallow, great tit, greenfinch and wood pigeon – but this will obviously vary according to the time of year – and also as the area becomes established).

Walk through Cowslips as the right lake is

Black Sheep Brewery, Masham

skirted. Cross a stile and turn left along a fence (parallel to lake). Towards the field end turn right to follow a fence line. The path is not easy to find from this point, but continue over a fence and go through a left wall to turn right. Follow this line to a track leading to Low Mains Farm. Don't turn right with the track but continue northwards to High Mains Cottages. When the 1st house is reached on the right turn left on the farm road and head south. The track soon bends right (to the west).

Gravel pits have been extended northwards over a vast area – the path follows a left hedge just north of the pits. Keep following the track until a pond is reached on the left. Go through a gate and turn right alongside a wall, with the small hummocks of Wind Hills to the left.

A small wood is passed to the right. Follow the wall/hedge until it ends, then carry on the same line. At a broken wall turn slightly right to head for Low Ellington hamlet (to arrive at the road at the south end of houses).

Turn right on the road which quickly becomes a farm track as the hamlet is left behind. The track bears right and left then ends. Carry on in a straight line over a stile and keep the fence to the right. There are a lot of grouse in this area. A small pond eventually appears on the far fence side and a gate is crossed in a fence. This is quickly followed by a stile after 30 metres on the right. Pass left of a limekiln and follow a fence for 200 m, then begin to bear right to reach a gate and the river. Grey wagtails are frequent visitors to the river.

Follow the riverside initially, then cut off a bend before rejoining. Pass ruined Squirrel Bank Farm, then swing up to its access track. Turn right on the track and follow it as it swings right to Kilgram Grange (a farm). The track carries on to join Kilgram Lane. Turn left on the lane until it turns sharp left. At this point go straight ahead, past a lodge, onto a drive through Jervaulx Park estate. The

Squirrel Bank Ruined Farm
170
High Mains Cottage
396
169
River Ure
To Low Mains Farm
Difficult Area
Pool
395
Mar Field
River Ure
River Ure
Bank Villa
MASHAM
GR SE 224 809
168

River Ure
398
LOW ELLINGTON
397
Wind Hills
Wood
169

drive is planted with Maple and Oak to add interest, before the abbey ruins are reached.

Jervaulx, Fountains and Rievaulx Abbeys form the Holy Trinity of Yorkshire. Jervaulx (pronounced 'Yervo', a name derived from the River Ure) was founded in 1156 by the white- robed Cistercian monks. The monks were forbidden to eat the cheese which they produced, but this was sold and became the original Wensleydale Cheese. They are also thought to have bred the Swaledale Sheep breed. The last abbott, Adam Sedbar, was taken to London and hanged at Tyburn for joining the Prilgrimage of Grace against Henry VIII. The extensive abbey was demolished in 1537 but there are still good remains, especially of the monks' dormitory. The estate and abbey are privately owned by the Burdon family.

Go past the ruins to reach the road and Jervaulx Hall (the abbey tea rooms are 30m left on the road).

Turn right on the road for 250m to cross Harker Beck and turn right immediately after the beck onto a farm track, to rejoin the river. Turn left along the riverbank and follow this all the way to Cover Bridge. Go onto the road and cross the bridge, then turn left past the 1674 Coverbridge Inn. Just past the inn and a bungalow turn left through a stile to regain the bank of the River Cover. The path soon enters a separate riverside path, which has quickly become a 'nature reserve'. Count the fields on the right and part way through the 6th field go right over a stile. Pass diagonally across the field to meet a wall which is followed uphill straight away from the river. A walled track is soon reached (with a name – Straight Lane). Just before this access track joins the A6108 road there is a

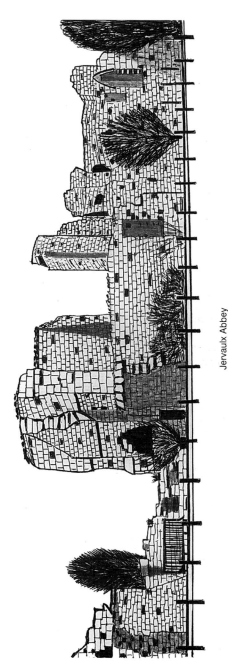

Jervaulx Abbey

stile on the left, which is taken to follow a right wall/fence. When a cross wall is reached turn left for 100m, then through a

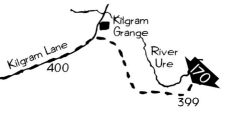

stile on the right. Follow a right fence, then go over a stile between hedges. A cross track is soon reached. Turn right to pass the castle to reach the centre of Middleham.

Middleham Castle was built on an earlier Motte and Bailey castle site. The castle guarded the Richmond to Skipton road. Its oldest part is the mas-sive 1170 rectangular keep, which is one of the largest in England. This was the baronial seat of the Neville family. Richard, Duke of Gloucester, came here to be schooled. It was here that Richard met Anne Neville (who was the daughter of Warwick the Kingmaker), and already a widow at the age of 16. The couple married in 1474 and the castle was part of Anne's dowry. Life here was uneventful until Edward IV died and Richard became King Richard III in 1483. The castle remains are now owned by English Heritage and open to the public from March to October.

Just over 1km to the northeast lies the village of Spennithorne whose church featured as *'Darrowby church'* in the BBC TV series *'All Creatures Great and Small'*.

Take the road north out of the village, turning left into an entry road leading to the church of St Alkelda which is dedicated to a Saxon princess who was strangled in 800 by 2 Danish women. Walk through the graveyard and out through a stile leading into a field. At the field end turn right and cross an access road, then immediately left to bypass a small housing estate. Cross a stile into a field and follow the very sub-

A different kind of gate fastener

Middleham Castle

stantial left wall. Go through a further stile and turn right for 150m – then left (don't go through the stile ahead). Follow a right wall/fence, near the end of which a stile is taken on the right. Turn left through this

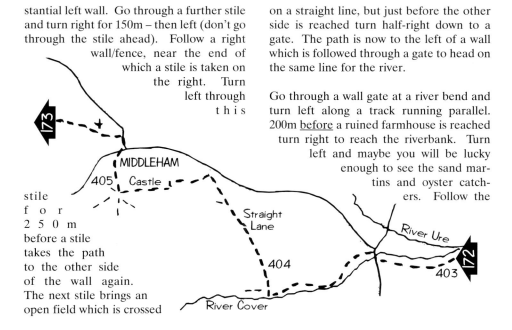

stile for 250m before a stile takes the path to the other side of the wall again. The next stile brings an open field which is crossed

on a straight line, but just before the other side is reached turn half-right down to a gate. The path is now to the left of a wall which is followed through a gate to head on the same line for the river.

Go through a wall gate at a river bend and turn left along a track running parallel. 200m before a ruined farmhouse is reached turn right to reach the riverbank. Turn left and maybe you will be lucky enough to see the sand martins and oyster catchers. Follow the bank all the way to the beautiful 4 arch Wensley Bridge, which is crossed to enter Wensley. Turn right at the church 407 onto the Middleham Road, which soon passes over a small stream. Turn immediately left at this point onto a narrow lane. The lane turns right then bears left. At this point go through the 2nd gate on the right to cross a field to a stile 50m from the right corner. Follow the right fence through the 1st field. In the 2nd field aim for the left of a wood opposite, to go over a stile and follow the wood edge, then through another stile shortly afterwards on the right. The path now goes through Leyburn Old Green Field (a Yorkshire Naturalist Trust Nature Reserve). Follow the left wall through a field, then in the next field head straight across to the opposite stile. Cross a small field, to go through a stile and turn left. At last Leyburn can be seen.

Turn right before the next wall and follow this line through a large number of fields and stiles, but always keeping to the right of a hedge/fence. Finally an open field is reached and crossed slightly left to reach the railway line. The line used to run from Northallerton to Garsdale (on the Settle to Carlisle line), with typical running times being Northallerton to Leyburn 42 min: Leyburn to Hawes 36 min. The track still operates for the occasional freight load up to Redmire only. Cross the track, then 2 fields to reach the A684 road. Turn right on the pavement to arrive at the centre of Leyburn. The village has a large square and a number of inns and tea rooms where sustenance can be obtained before continuing the walk. Francis I'Anson was born here on the 17th October 1766 – she was the sweet lass of Richmond Hill in the song of the same name. The village also has the distinction of having a Violin-making workshop which is worth a visit.

River Ure — 174 — 407 — 406 — 173 — MIDDLEHAM — LEYBURN GR SE III 905 — A684 — 410 — 409 — WENSLEY — 408 — 174 — Wensley Bridge — A684

THIRTY
Leyburn - Marrick
(11.3 miles or 18.1 km)

This part of the GEW is almost as difficult as section 6 in terms of route finding. There is also a sting in the tail! From the main square of Leyburn walk past the side of the Bolton Arms Inn and the Dalesman's Club, and into Shawl Mews. At the end of

Quarry

Leyburn
Shawl   4ll

t h e short road turn left and right onto the Shawl. What is a Shawl? In this case it's a great limestone ridge overlooking the Ure valley to the south, and Wensleydale to the west. In 1587 Mary, Queen of Scots, escaped from Bolton Castle (where she had been kept as a prisoner). She was recaptured here, but during the incident her shawl fell to the ground. The ridge has been known as the Shawl ever since.

A plantation is soon reached on the left and the obvious path is followed along the ridge edge (with a large limestone quarry to the

right). The path switches to the left of a wall for a long walk along the ridge. When the wood ends cross 2 stiles and turn downhill for 1 field, go over stiles then bear right across a level field. Cross another stile and go through the next field towards Gillfield Wood. A path crossroad is met at the wood's edge. Go through a gate and enter the wood. Don't turn left, but go ahead to cross a stream. There are some remains in this area of a wire hawser aerial ropeway. The wood is a 'rabbit warren' of old workings and paths. Bend slightly, but ignore all turn-offs to press on ahead as straight as possible, to exit the wood at a stile. Cross a field to reach a minor road. Turn right on the road; with Shining Crane's-bill, Greater Celandine and Ivy-leaved Toadflax lining the road edge. The road soon reaches a road junction at Preston-under-Scar. Some 3km west of this point is Bolton Castle (where Queen Mary had been imprisoned) if a diversion is fancied.

LEYBURN
GR SE lll 905

A684

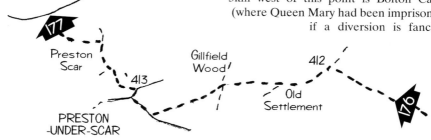

Preston
Scar

4l3

PRESTON
-UNDER-SCAR

Gillfield
Wood

4l2

Old
Settlement

The castle is a fortified manor house built in the 14th century by Richard Scrope, chancellor to Richard II. The castle was held by the Royalists in the English Civil War, and only surrendered to Cromwell's troops after a year-long siege.

Turn right on a road for 200m, then left on a farm track for 30m. Cross a cattlegrid and turn half-right to pass left of a water tank. Climb to a stile near the walled wood and continue up on an enclosed path, to reach Preston Scar. There is yet another disused quarry

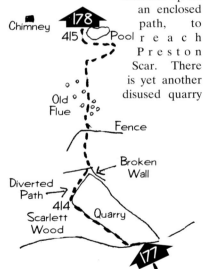

to the right. This is a much lesser ridge than Leyburn Shawl. Cross 2 fields to reach a road. This is a tank turning area, with the massive Redmire quarry opposite. The path here has been much altered since the quarry opened. Follow the signposted diversion to the left of the quarry access road, which takes the path along a continuation of Preston Scar, above Scarlet Wood. The path continues to the limit of the extended quarry, then goes through a fence

and turns right. No doubt the path line will alter again as the quarry extends. The problem now is to get back to the original path line! From the path line a tumbledown wall can be seen some 200m ahead, with a signed gate slightly left. Head for this and pass through the gate into a newly planted tree area, which is passed through and a stile taken on the far side giving access to open moorland.

Ahead can be seen an old chimney at the abandoned Cobscar Mill. These moors are dotted with ruins of mine shafts, engine houses and smelting mills for the lead mines which were worked until the late 19th century. The yellow flowered Mountain Pansy thrives in the area, since it prefers upland pastures and rocky

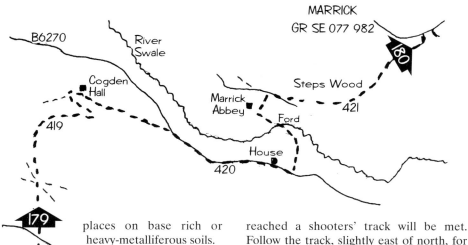

MARRICK
GR SE 077 982

B6270

River
Swale

Cogden
Hall

Steps Wood

180

Marrick
Abbey

421

Ford

419

House

420

179

places on base rich or heavy-metalliferous soils.

A i m initially for the distant chimney, but then start to bear right to discover an old flue (a long wide line of stones leading to the chimney). Cross the flue and aim for the old tips ahead to reach a large pond some 400m right of the chimney. At the time of writing (1997) the way north from this point is not easy.

Head directly north from the left side of the pond, through Heather to a tumbledown wall some 150m away. When the wall is

reached a shooters' track will be met. Follow the track, slightly east of north, for approximately 700m. The track reaches an area of old scrapes and workings and meets a track junction with a footpath sign pointing left!

Turn immediately left on the signed right of way. Redmire Moor is to the left and Preston Moor to the right. This is an e x t r e m e l y desolate and dreary area. The track heads off west to reach some grouse butts and then bears right. Follow the

Snowden Man boundary stone

track between peat hillocks up to a slight ridge. From this point take a compass bearing and head due north (at one point the chimney can be seen behind – due south and confirming the correct direction). Keep heading north until a wall corner is seen ahead. Head straight for the corner of the broken wall. Here is the very weathered inscribed Snowden Man boundary stone (where did the name come from?). The length of Swaledale is now exposed below, with moorland as far as the eye can see. There is also a deathly silence, not surprising in this awful place.

Cross the wall and fence near the wall corner and head downhill through Heather. The landscape is featureless, but bear slightly right to finally reach the start of a small stream in Glead Gill. Cross the stream and keep more or less downhill along the right bank until the old buildings of Grinton Smelting Mill are finally reached. There are disused tips/levels/shafts/scrapes all over these moors dug as men searched for lead many years ago.

From the buildings turn right and climb the old flue line to reach the 'peak' of Sharrow Hill. Descend to the left of the hill to pick up a bridleway leading to a minor road 250m away. Cross the road and continue on the clear bridleway. Grinton village can be seen below in Swaledale, with

its splendid church known as the Cathedral of the Dales. Go through 2 fields, meet a wall and swing right through a gate. Follow the track as it maintains height. Cogden Hall is passed below to the left, then turn sharp left on the track to descend to the hall. Turn right and right again around outbuildings onto the track in front of the hall.

Go straight ahead through 2 gates into a field. Follow the right wall through the 1st field, then through a gate which switches the wall to the left. Field Rush is a very prolific plant in the fields in springtime. Go over a stile into an open field and on to reach the B6270 road. Turn right on the road for almost 1 km, until one field past a house on the left, then turn left through a gate into a green lane. Another 1 km on the road would have brought you to Ellerton Priory, established in 1227 for Cistercian nuns, but now a sparse ruin.

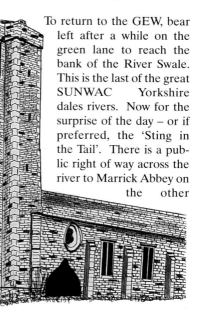

To return to the GEW, bear left after a while on the green lane to reach the bank of the River Swale. This is the last of the great SUNWAC Yorkshire dales rivers. Now for the surprise of the day – or if preferred, the 'Sting in the Tail'. There is a public right of way across the river to Marrick Abbey on the other

Marrick Abbey

Ford over River Swale

side, but no stepping stones or bridge. The river must be forded (nearest bridges are over 2km to the west or 5km east). How the river is forded is left entirely up to you! Bare feet are best, but the stones are very slippy—so the decision may be boots for safety! The County Council do hope to install stepping stones when funds permit. Once the other bank is reached, and the ordeal overcome, carry on up to a gate and round the left of a house to reach Marrick Abbey. The abbey was founded by Roger de Aske for the Benedictine order in the 12th century. The 'church' is in good repair and now used as a church youth centre.

Go round the abbey to reach the metalled access road on its north side. Turn right (joining the Coast to Coast path) until 50m beyond a cattle grid, then turn half-left through a stile up to Steps Wood. This is the ancient route from Marrick to the Abbey and is cobbled/flagged all the way through the wood. Both Water and Wood Avens will be found in the wood. Beyond the wood follow the right wall through 2 fields to a lane leading into Marrick.

THIRTY ONE
Marrick - Barnard Castle
(22.0 miles or 35.2 km)

This is the longest GEW section, but is a quite stunning and rewarding walk.

Bear left to reach the 'main road' in Marrick near a telephone kiosk and post box. Turn right to a T junction. Turn right again (signed C to C walk) to pass 'The School House' and 'Park Lodge', then left onto an access track which reduces to a path after 50m. Go ahead on an obvious path, through a large number of fields and stiles, until the access track 200m east of Nun Cote Nook Farm is reached. Turn right for 30m to a wall end. Turn left to follow a wall, making for the right side of a barn. Cross the next field diagonally right, go through a gate and follow the left wall to reach the house at Ellers. Turn left around the house and cross Ellers Beck. Proceed across the next 2 fields to the left side of Hollins Farm Wood and reach a farm track. Turn half-right through a fence, maintaining this line through 3 fields. Aim for a house on the road at Hardstiles Top. The Coast to Coast goes right here on its way to Richmond, but the GEW turns left on the road for 150m, then through a gate on the right. Head half-right, to the left side of a wood behind a house, go over 2 stiles and follow the left fence downhill to Skelton Lane.

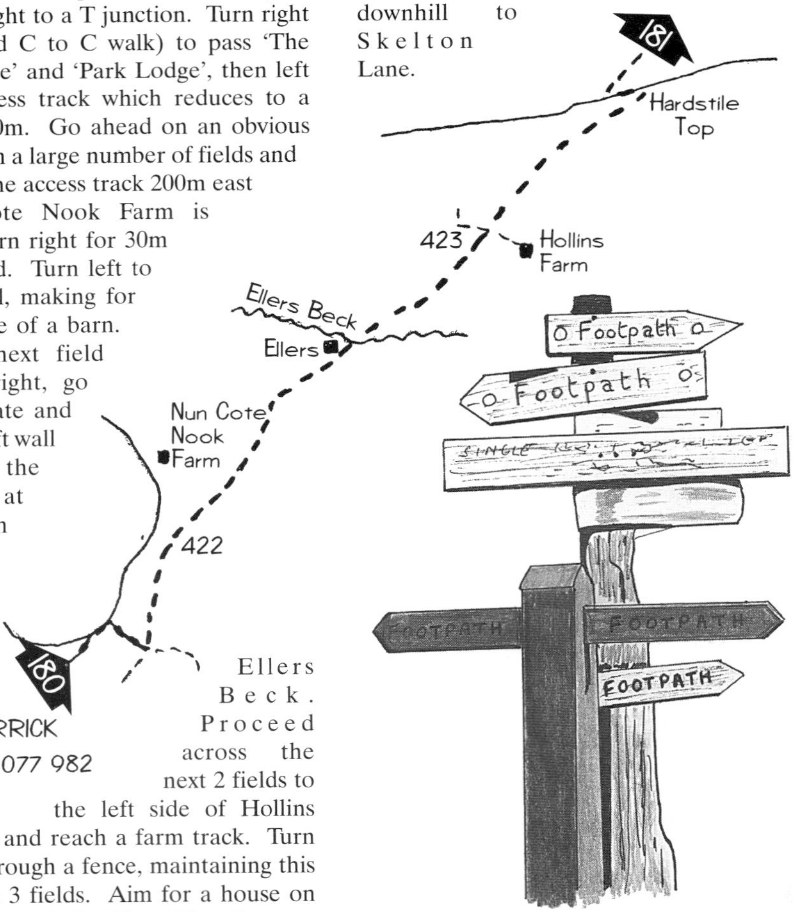

Ellers Beck

Ellers

Nun Cote
Nook
Farm

422

MARRICK
GR SE 077 982

423

Hollins
Farm

Hardstile
Top

Near Nun Cote Nook Farm

Cross the road, go through a small gate (to right of a house drive) and down to the medieval Pillimire Bridge. Under the bridge can be seen a joint where the bridge was widened from the original packhorse width. The mill has gone, but there is still a waterwheel here on the Marske Beck. Turn left along the beck to pass through part of Clints Wood and reach the 'road' at Clints. Turn left on the track through the delightful wood which is followed all the way to Orgate Farm. Clints Scar towers above to the northeast. Just before the farm turn left on the track down to the footbridge over Marske Beck. Follow the track for 100m to beyond a barn, then turn right and follow the right wall until Telfit Farm is almost reached (the path has been moved from that shown on OS maps). Go through the gate on the track some 100m west of the farm, and immediately leave the track to follow a right wall. Pass through a fallen

wall and bend left as the path descends to the water's edge, but follow a level some 20m up from the beck until a beckside wall/fence can be followed to the hamlet of Helwith.

Cross the beck by the footbridge and turn left in front of a barn, to follow the access road as it zig-zags uphill and goes through a gate to the right of a barn. Leave the 'road' and follow a left wall, then walk parallel to the road for 300m until a final wall, before Holgate Moor. Head off half-left along the wall. The farm road from Lummar House is joined for 100m, then left to continue following the convenient wall. The area to the right is called Sail How. Keep following the wall until it bends sharply left. At this point head straight ahead, across a farm road, to reach the left of a wall of a long rectangular wall system. At the end of the field system keep straight on, skirting Holgate How to

Mole cemetery

Pillimire Bridge

the right (437m), to reach more walls. There is a field system to the left (downhill). The wall should not be crossed but followed right until the access track for West House is reached. The house is some 150m beyond the wall. Go through the gate on the track and head across the moor 50m up above the house, on a northwest direction to meet a tarmac farm access track (to Kexwith Farm down in the valley to the left). Turn left on the track for 100m, then leave the track half-right (on a compass bearing of 335 degrees) to cross the Heather-clad Holgate Moor.

After 1km the valley of Kexwith Beck is seen ahead, but do not lose height and gradually swing right across the track-

less moor. The joining of the 2 valleys of Arndale Beck and Arndale Springs now becomes obvious. Maintain height above Arndale Springs and, at last, a wall is seen running along the valley bottom. Still maintain height and gradually converge with the wall, which is then followed until the valley almost ends and the wall turns right. Pass through a gate near the wall corner and head slightly left (335 degrees compass) along a line of grouse butts. The butts are on the line of what remains of the valley just left behind. The route now runs some 50m parallel to the right of the butts and reaches a cross wall. The wall is the boundary between North Yorkshire and County Durham.

From the wall carry on a faint track going

half-right which soon reaches old scrape holes. Turn half-left and soon the valley of Osmaril Gill starts on the right. Keep following the track as it bears left, with the ridge of Cross Gill on the right (437m). Teesdale can now be seen to the north. A crest is reached and 'The Stang' forest is laid out below. The perimeter fence is very angular. On the far side of Cross Gill is a 'cliff' face and as this appears to end, turn right and head down towards the forest. The perimeter fence runs north, then northeast, then north again. The gate required to gain access is

near the right side of the 'northeast bit'. There are moves to erect wind turbines on Cross Gill! 150m west of the fence corner is the gate giving access to a wide forest trail. The trail soon joins a 'forest road' which is followed left, to pass 2 walled fields on the right. Turn half-right beyond the walls, still on the 'road'. The road bends left, but carry on straight ahead on a trail to meet a minor road (from West Hope to East Hope).

Turn right on the road to reach East Hope hamlet. The road swings left past East Hope House, then after 70m turn left off the road at a bend. Go over a stream and locked gate. Head north to find a stone stile and the Gutters Bridge foot-bridge over Scargill Beck.

Cross the field ahead on a straight line to reach a gate in the far fence. Cross to left of a barn in the next field to the footbridge over Gregory Beck, then slightly left to a gate. Follow the right fence uphill in the next field, to turn right through a gate and follow a left wall. Go

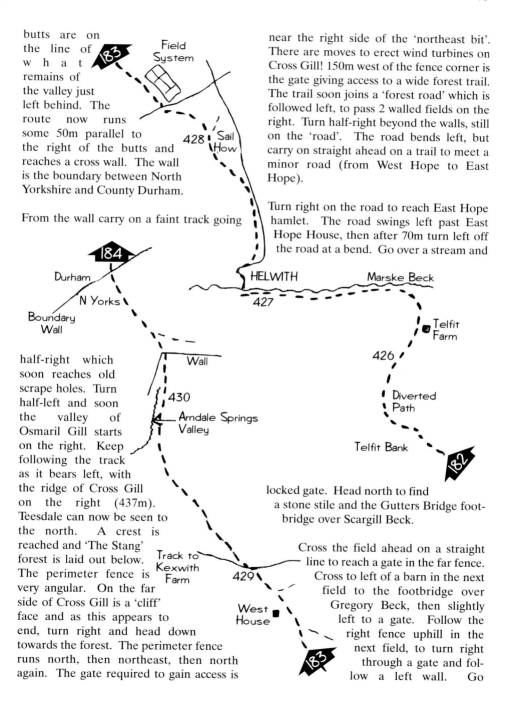

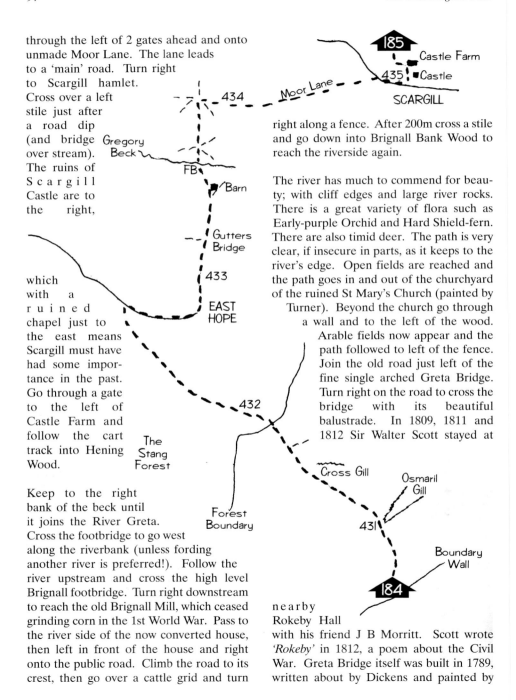

through the left of 2 gates ahead and onto unmade Moor Lane. The lane leads to a 'main' road. Turn right to Scargill hamlet. Cross over a left stile just after a road dip (and bridge over stream). The ruins of Scargill Castle are to the right,

which with a ruined chapel just to the east means Scargill must have had some importance in the past. Go through a gate to the left of Castle Farm and follow the cart track into Hening Wood.

Keep to the right bank of the beck until it joins the River Greta. Cross the footbridge to go west along the riverbank (unless fording another river is preferred!). Follow the river upstream and cross the high level Brignall footbridge. Turn right downstream to reach the old Brignall Mill, which ceased grinding corn in the 1st World War. Pass to the river side of the now converted house, then left in front of the house and right onto the public road. Climb the road to its crest, then go over a cattle grid and turn

right along a fence. After 200m cross a stile and go down into Brignall Bank Wood to reach the riverside again.

The river has much to commend for beauty; with cliff edges and large river rocks. There is a great variety of flora such as Early-purple Orchid and Hard Shield-fern. There are also timid deer. The path is very clear, if insecure in parts, as it keeps to the river's edge. Open fields are reached and the path goes in and out of the churchyard of the ruined St Mary's Church (painted by Turner). Beyond the church go through a wall and to the left of the wood. Arable fields now appear and the path followed to left of the fence. Join the old road just left of the fine single arched Greta Bridge. Turn right on the road to cross the bridge with its beautiful balustrade. In 1809, 1811 and 1812 Sir Walter Scott stayed at

nearby Rokeby Hall with his friend J B Morritt. Scott wrote 'Rokeby' in 1812, a poem about the Civil War. Greta Bridge itself was built in 1789, written about by Dickens and painted by

Turner. The Morritt Arms Inn is built on the site of a Roman fort.

50m beyond the bridge turn left over a stile and head for the farm track alongside the river, to pass under the A66 road. Go ahead to the right of a fence and climb to the right side of Mortham Wood. When the wood ends carry on the same line along the remains of a hedge. At the end of this 'field' is a barn, where a left turn is made onto a farm track to regain the wood. Bear right with the track to reach Mortham Tower, built by a 15th century Lord of

Rokeby when his home was destroyed by Scots invaders and now a private residence. Turn right in front of the 'Hall' gates and follow the drive to cross Dairy Bridge at the 'Meeting of the Waters' of the Rivers Greta and Tees.

The drive now becomes a tarmac road which goes west to join a larger minor road. Just before the road junction turn right onto a wooded riverside path. The wood is replaced by fields and then a wood again. The riverside banks of the Tees are comprised of massive rocks. Egglestone Abbey Bridge is reached – a magnificent structure built in 1773 over the Abbey Gorge. Cross the bridge but don't take the

Brignall Mill

436

437

River Greta

Hening Wood

186

185

Bowes Museum

path going left immediately after the bridge, nor the next path. Go left on the path opposite the drive of Mains House, which is followed on a level above the river. The ruins of the 12th century Premonstratensian Egglestone Abbey , founded by Ralph de Malton, are on the other side of the river. Cross the sewage treatment works drive to continue following the left hedge. In the next field, as a stile is reached on the left, bear right up the field. Pass the rugby pitch to the left

St Mary's
Church
(Ruin)

438

and press ahead going towards the wall on the right. Bowes Museum is to the right.

Greta Bridge

439

A66

187

The Bowes House is a French style chateau built in 1869/75 by John Bowes (a wealthy local magnate) for his French wife Josephine. The art collection is housed in 40 rooms and is one of the most original, dramatic and finest in Great Britain.

When the wall ends turn right along a passage to reach Westwick Road. Turn left along Newgate to reach Barnard Castle. The town has 2 notable claims to fame.

a. The castle was built by Bernard Baliol, whose father had aided William the Conqueror. His descendants include a

Mortham Tower

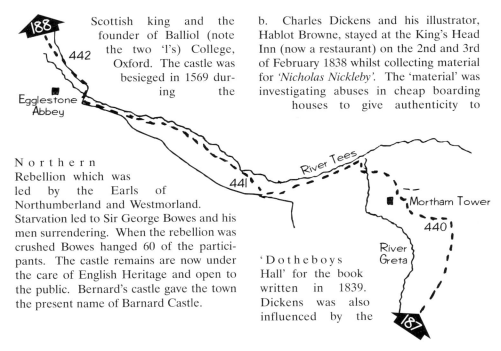

Scottish king and the founder of Balliol (note the two 'l's) College, Oxford. The castle was besieged in 1569 during the

Northern Rebellion which was led by the Earls of Northumberland and Westmorland. Starvation led to Sir George Bowes and his men surrendering. When the rebellion was crushed Bowes hanged 60 of the participants. The castle remains are now under the care of English Heritage and open to the public. Bernard's castle gave the town the present name of Barnard Castle.

b. Charles Dickens and his illustrator, Hablot Browne, stayed at the King's Head Inn (now a restaurant) on the 2nd and 3rd of February 1838 whilst collecting material for *'Nicholas Nickleby'*. The 'material' was investigating abuses in cheap boarding houses to give authenticity to

'Dotheboys Hall' for the book written in 1839. Dickens was also influenced by the

Egglestone Abbey Bridge

Masham Market Square

Greta Bridge

town's clockmakers shop in choosing the title *'Master Humphrey's Clock'* written in 1840 for his new weekly in which *'The Old Curiosity Shop'* (1840) and *'Barnaby Rudge'* (1840/1) appeared.

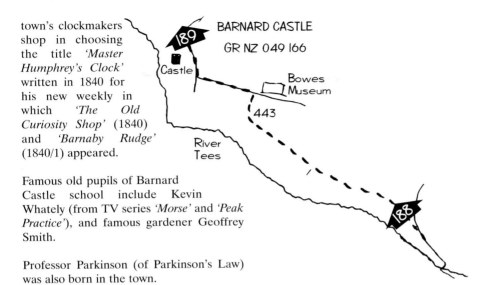

Famous old pupils of Barnard Castle school include Kevin Whately (from TV series *'Morse'* and *'Peak Practice'*), and famous gardener Geoffrey Smith.

Professor Parkinson (of Parkinson's Law) was also born in the town.

Old railway viaduct and River Tees

River East Allen at Oakpool

Hamsterley Forest

From the town centre walk along Flatts Road, passing the Tourist Information Centre, to its junction with Vere Road. Turn left and continue past the end of Raby Avenue down a small 'No Entry' continuation of Vere Road. Turn right after 50m onto a path. After a further 150m turn left through a stile into a Woodland Trust wood. Descend the path through the wood to arrive at a weir on the River Tees. Turn right on the riverside path, to pass a footbridge (don't cross) and follow the river on a broad track. The track soon bends with a footbridge over Black Beck. The Tees is by far the widest and largest river encountered since the Severn was left at Shrewsbury. The path along the Tees is a delightful walk. After a while climb up to pass the remains of what must have been a magnificent railway viaduct. Barnard Castle used to be a busy railway junction. Trains ran from BC to Lartington, then turned south to Bowes and west to Barras, Kirkby Stephen, Smardale, Ravenstonedale, Gaisgill and Tebay (1 hour 32 mins running time). Just west of the river a line split from the above ran to

Cotherstone, Romaldkirk, Mickleton and Middleton-in-Teesdale (22 minutes). East of BC the line again split with tracks to Bishop Auckland (31 minutes) and Darlington (40 minutes).

As well as more common flowers this walk along the Tees is marked by discoveries of Globeflower (only found north from North Staffs), Early-purple Orchid, Field Madder and the beautifully scented Woodruff.

Ascend a flight of steps at the river bend apex just before Tees Bank. The path eventually leaves the wood to reach a wall gate. Through the gate follow the right wall through the field for 150m, then turn right through another gate to climb through the wood for 150m. Turn left at the ridge gate to follow the top side of the wood through fields and gates. East Holme House Farm is over to the right as the path continues along the wood edge to a high stile giving access to the left of West Holme House Farm. Pass to the left of the farm wall and cross a stile to follow the farm track across a field. A 2nd field takes the path back to the wood's edge and in the 3rd field a stile takes the path between a wood and fence, to curve right along a limb of the wood and a small ravine. Cross a footbridge over a stream and turn half-right to climb to a walled gate. Through the gate head across the field to the right side of the wood ahead. Halfway through the last field, before the one containing Low Shipley Farm, go over a stile on the left to descend to a field alongside the river.

Pass the junction of the River Balder (on the far side) to reach a footbridge over the Tees. DON'T CROSS (unless you wish to visit Cotherstone, once famous for cheese making). Think carefully at this point and turn half-right at the end of the bridge, to soon reach a well used track heading up through the trees to a caravan park. As soon as you reach the caravans cross straight through (to the left of a toilet block) on a path which climbs through Gorse bushes. Go over a stile and carry on the same line across a small field and over a stone stile leading into a wood. Turn right to walk through the wood and cross a stile to exit. Turn left over a wooden bridge and follow the left bank of a small stream. The path rejoins the wood, then splits over a stile. Follow the left fence/wood for 1 field and 1 stile, then turn half-right to follow a fence line for 300m until it turns half-right. Leave the track at this point and head straight across the field to a stile. Eggleston can now be seen ahead. Carry on the same line for 250m heading for the left of a solitary Oak tree and then on to a stile 50m to its far left. Over this bear half-right to a stile giving access to Raygill Beck. Cross this and head for a gate 50m to the right side of East Barnley Farm. Cross a field to the farmhouse and farm drive. Do not fol-

River Tees

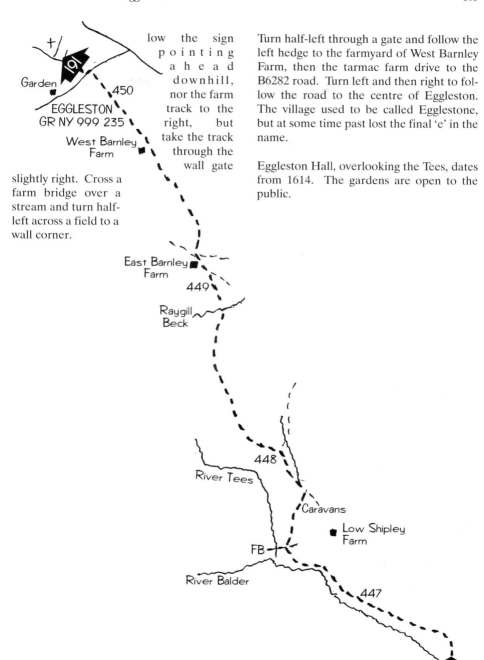

low the sign pointing ahead downhill, nor the farm track to the right, but take the track through the wall gate

slightly right. Cross a farm bridge over a stream and turn half-left across a field to a wall corner.

Turn half-left through a gate and follow the left hedge to the farmyard of West Barnley Farm, then the tarmac farm drive to the B6282 road. Turn left and then right to follow the road to the centre of Eggleston. The village used to be called Egglestone, but at some time past lost the final 'e' in the name.

Eggleston Hall, overlooking the Tees, dates from 1614. The gardens are open to the public.

THIRTY THREE
Eggleston - Stanhope
(16.8 miles or 26.9 km)

300m from the junction of the B6282 with the B6281 is a small road on the right. Walk up this road and pass Holy Trinity Church on the left. 75m past the church turn left on an access road for 50m then go through a small gate into a field. Follow the right wall to cross an old clapper bridge and climb a few steps, then cross a field with a hedge to the left and cross a stile into a 2nd field. There are medieval cultivation terraces to the right. Near the end of the field climb the terraces up to the wall on the right. Pass through a stile in a transverse wall (blocked in 1997). In the next field follow the right wall and just after the next gate bear right with the wall to a small gated stile. On the same line cross a small field to find a gate and turn left on an access track which leads to a minor road. Turn right on the road until it meets the B6278.

Turn left on the road and go around the bend which takes the road over the valley of the Blackton Beck. There are 2 bungalows on the right. Just past the 2nd (Braeside) turn right through a gate onto a farm track. The twin peaks to the left are the 'Knotts' (440m). After 300m the path splits. Go ahead through a gate to follow the fence alongside Blackton Beck. The fence ends

Knotts near Eggleston

at a wall gate. Pass through and turn half-left, passing sheepfolds. Follow the wide bridleway as it starts to cross Eggleston Common Moor, soon passing a disused overgrown small reservoir to the left. About 1km further brings grouse butts to the left. Watch for a marker pole at this point. The main track bears right downhill to a shooters' shelter, but a bridleway track leaves diagonally left on a distinct path through Heather. A rise on the path gives the 1st glimpse of Hamsterley Forest, a 2,500 hectare forest.

wards and north to the Weir. Beyond the burn climb a short rise through a small young plantation. After 250m the track bends slightly right across the very beginning of a Quarter Burn tributary. At this point a decision must be made! There is an obvious track still to be followed going northeast. Another path starts at this point and a depression can be seen going through the Heather straight ahead. This 'hidden' path is the one required, but is extremely difficult going. Until the required route is cleared discretion may dictate following the obvious (and waymarked) path for 1.2km to reach the perimeter of the forest.

If on the alternative then just before the forest is met cross Smithy Hirst Sike and turn left on a forest road for some 400m, until 2 small pools on the sike are seen down to the left. Near the pools can be seen a footbridge – which carries

Map labels: 192, 452, Blackton Beck, 451, PH, EGGLESTON GR NY 999 235, 191, 193, Slate Ledge, Sheepfold, 453, 192

Forests are an anathema to most walkers. They give a sense of imprisonment, more so with the dense conifer plantations much loved by the old Forestry Commission. Unfortunately there are a number to be traversed, this one in County Durham and the rest in Northumberland. The best advice that can be offered is to 'grin and bear it', and remember that they do not go on for ever, even though it seems like it at times!

This area is known as Slate Ledge and is the watershed between water flowing south to the Tees and north to the Weir. The track descends slightly to pass through the Quarter Burn flowing east-

the 'hidden' path which should have been followed in the first place! Turn right at this point to enter the forest on a forest road. In 300m there is a T junction on the road. Cross the road and go straight ahead on what is now just a forest trail. The trail is usually wet and has been deeply rutted by overuse of mountain bikes. The best one can say is that this forest has been opened to the public for pleasure, and this is a bridleway – so bikers are quite legitimate users. The track deteriorates further but is obvious to follow for 800m to reach another broad forest road. There is a Public Right Of Way heading northeast from this point for nearly 4km to the 'Meeting of the Grains' but this is completely tree planted and impassable (in 1997). Therefore the GEW has been

devised over a different route. You were warned that forest walking is different!

goes left soon after this and continue uphill. Middle Redford hamlet is across the fields to the right. Reach the summit of Potato Hill with a junction of 5 tracks.

Turn 90 degrees left onto a wide forest path for 200m to reach the left side of the wood at a wall stile. Cross the stile to enter Hamsterley Common – a vast moorland. Follow a faint track (compass 295 degrees) and after 200m find 2 cairns marking the start of an obvious path. Follow the path as it goes along a level contour with Ayhope Beck down in a small valley to the right. Curlews will normally be seen. After some distance the path suddenly becomes a farm track, which is followed to the 'Meeting of the Grains'. This is a point where South Grain Beck and North Grain Beck meet to form Ayhope Beck. The track fords South Grain Beck – and ends. Head uphill away from the beck to pass to the right of a just discernable old wall enclosure. Carry on to aim for a wide

Because of the above, having reached the aforementioned forest road, turn right for 200m then left at a junction for a 4km walk on this well-engineered but flat and boring route, through the length of Hamsterley Forest. Eventually a forest crossroad is reached. Turn left for 200m. The road turns sharp left, but at this point go straight ahead on a path to the left of The Grove House. Pass the house to reach a footbridge over Euden Beck. Cross the bridge, ignoring Rothbury Forest Enterprise signed paths which go right and left, to head uphill on a track. At last there are a few broad-leaved trees. After 300m the wood on the right ends to give views of open fields again! Eudenbank house to the left is soon passed. Ignore the track which

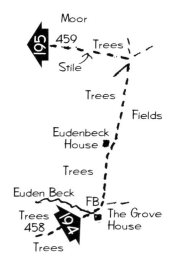

gap between an abandoned Hawthorn hedge to the left and a stand of Birch trees to the right. At the end of the left 'hedge' follow the line of an ancient ditch to reach a fence and stile. You now enter Pikestone Fell.

Still follow the ditch line for 50m (the embankment top was clearly once topped by a wall). Bear left on a path on a level above what is left of the trees. Cross a side beck feeder after 150m and then carry on to reach the

Allotment House

FP and wall

462

Trig Point 387m

FP and wall

junction of North Grain Beck and Steel Beck. Cross North Grain Beck and head up a path which disappears after 50m. The route ahead is now across barren unmarked territory – which is also absolutely featureless!

Head approximately northwest (330 degrees compass) for 1.5km until finally, with luck, a trig point is sighted. The Ordnance Survey no longer need these now they have GPS satellites, but please don't get rid of them! The trig point could be a life saver on this very barren moor. It is also the summit of Pikestone Fell at 387m (although there is no summit as such, just the highest point of the

Pikestone Fell

461

North Grain Beck

Fence Line ➔

South Grain Beck

Ayhope Beck

460

Hamsterley Common

moor). From the trig point head northwest (310 degrees compass) across the moor for 350m to reach a wall. What a relief to have found a way to this point! With luck you will arrive at a gate and signpost (for Weardale Way). Go through the gate and onto a track to reach the large Allotment House (now a barn), where the road now has a tarmac surface. Spirits improve as Weardale opens out ahead.

Follow the gated road for 1.8km to the hamlet of White Kirkley. Frosterley village is just 1km to the north, dating from 1183, with a name deriving from a *'forester's clearing'*. It had a 'Frosterley marble' quarry, some of which was used in Durham Cathedral. Not a true marble but stone which glistens because of the fossils it contains.

Beyond White Kirkley the road bears left for a further 500m to a road junction. Turn left and climb with the road to Hill End hamlet. Just past No 10 on the right (and before a telephone kiosk) turn right, go through a gate and turn right down a tarmac drive. Follow the drive as it bends left to the hamlet of Dryburn Side. Pass in front of Dryburnside Farm and go through a gate into a field. Turn half-right and head for the far right field corner. Pick up a farm track and turn left to cross a footbridge over Dry Burn (just before Peak Field Farm), and turn left alongside the burn through 3 wall stiles. After the 3rd stile bear slightly right to cross the field to a gate in the opposite fence/hedge. Cross a stile to the left of the gate and Stanhope is clear ahead.

In the next field pass to the right of old tips to a stile in front of the ruin of the engine house of an abandoned mine. Pass to the ruin's right and diagonally cross a field. After 150m cross a stile into a field on the right. Keep on the same line, almost following the left fence, to a stile in the far field side – then cross the next field along the same line to reach Cow Burn. There is a massive stretch of old tips to the left. Over the dried up burn head up a field to cross a wall stile. The next field has Lady's-mantle and Yellow-rattle which are good indicators of natural unfertilised fields.

A gate leads on to the bed of an old railway incline which used to transport the mined coal down to the main line track along Weardale. Cross the railbed and go through gates to the drive of Parson Byers Farm, which is crossed to a stile into a field. Follow the line of electricity poles down to terraced houses at Railway Terrace. Turn left along a road for 200m then right to cross bridges over the railway and the River Wear. 20m beyond the river turn left through a stile and follow this line to a rail level crossing.

197

464
HILL END

WHITE
KIRKLEY

463

Allotment
House

196

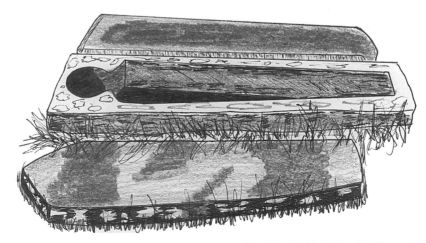

Frosterley Marble Coffins at St Thomas, Stangate

Rookhope Burn

The next field is the local football pitch, which is crossed diagonally right to another level crossing. The line is still occasionally used as a mineral line, but even this traffic seems to have almost ceased (in 1997). There used to be a regular passenger service from Bishop Auckland along the dale to Wearhead, calling at Frosterley, Stanhope, Eastgate, Westgate and St John's Chapel. It is hoped to re-establish a passenger service between Bishop Auckland and Stanhope in the near future. The path passes a row of houses and turns right into Market Place at Stanhope. (a Celtic name meaning *'stony valley'*).

The Romans decided that the Wear valley was very important since it carried their main supply line to Hadrian's Wall, Dere Street. They built a line of forts to protect this vital supply line. They also discovered the vast supply of lead which lay under the ground, and started the lead mining industry. In Roman times there were still many wild pigs in the area, and there is an altar in St Thomas's Church in Stanhope recording the victory of Caius over a legendary boar which gives an account of a boar of immense size, to which he erected the altar after discharging a vow to kill the beast.

William the Conqueror, aware of the threat to the north from the Scots, created a Prince Bishop (or Count Palatine) to enforce rule on the northern subjects. From 1080 until 1836 the Bishops of Durham were given power to enforce their rule over Durham and much of Northumberland. No less than 8 rectors of Stanhope became Prince Bishops of Durham. This shaped much of present day Weardale, with even field patterns developed to the Prince Bishops' scheme. King Stephen granted mineral rights in Weardale to Bishop de Puiset in 1160, and lead mining continued until comparatively recent times.

The Wear valley today is mainly in an Area of Outstanding Natural Beauty, and is England's largest AONB area. Stanhope is the 'capital' of the valley and has much to see. The market place dates from 1421 when a market charter was granted. The church of St Thomas was built in 1200, and near its entrance is a 1.5m tall petrified tree stump (of the sigillaria

STANHOPE
GR NY 997 392

98
467
466
Parson Byers
River Wear
Old Incline
Mine Tip
465
Peak Field Farm
Dryburn Side
97

Old Road to Riddlehamhope

Roman Fort at Vindolanda

species) which grew in the middle carboniferous period about 250 million years ago. When the tree vegetable matter decayed it was replaced by sand which has formed a perfect cast in hard ganister. To the left of the church porch is a collection of 13th century Frosterley marble coffins. Stanhope Hall is a mixture of dates (Medieval, Elizabethan and Jacobean), with remains

of lead and iron mines in Stanhope Dean (beyond the hall). There is a 1798 mock medieval castle.

Stanhope is an area where names change, marking early history. 'Beck' becomes 'Burn' north of this point. Other names also begin to change with 'Fells' becoming 'Laws' and 'Dene' replacing 'Gill'.

Bainbridge Chapel, Eastgate

THIRTY FOUR
Stanhope - Blanchland
(13.4 miles or 21.4 km)

Leave Stanhope along the A689 road going west from the Market Place. The Durham Dales & Craft Centre is on the right side (Tourist Information Centre and tea room). Continue along the road until Stanhope Hall is reached and turn left along the B6278 road opposite. This road leads to the medieval Stanhope Bridge over the Wear. Don't cross the river but leave the road at this point to carry on the track ahead. There is a flooded disused quarry to the right. Follow the riverside and cross the railway line and then follow the left fence/wall. The Wild Pansy enhances the riverside walk. The path is soon contained between the railway and the river for a pleasant riverside stretch. As the path nears Eastgate pass through a static caravan site. At the end of the site bear right on the site access drive to reach Hag Bridge (a modern replacement). Turn right on the minor road. Walk across the rail bridge, with the old Eastgate Station on the right, then carry on the road to turn left when it meets the A689 road.

Eastgate, founded by the Romans, is soon reached. Eastgate and Westgate towns mark the entrances to the Prince Bishops' great hunting park. The Blue Circle

Petrified tree, Stanhope

cement works dominates the town, but has kept the rail line open for mineral use this far up the dale. Just before the 1st road on the right is a replica 3rd century Roman altar, placed here by Durham County Council in 1969 to commemorate the finding of the original 300m north of this spot in 1869. The translation from the Latin reads *'Aurelius Quirinus,*

conveyor up to the quarry on Billing Hills, of the extensive Blue Circle Weardale Works. Go through the gate to the right of the farm onto a green path, which climbs a

Prefect,   set this up to the God Silvanus'. Silvanus was a Roman god of the woods and of hunting. Aurelius Quirinus was probably stationed at Lanchester as Prefect of Cohort 1 Lingonum (an infantry regiment) in the reign of   Emperor Gordian (AD   238   to   244).

terrace. There are plenty of wild flowers to delight the eye. Follow the left fence and keep on the same line when this ends. The path soon reaches the sparse Ambling Gate Bank Wood – a nice wood consisting of Dog Rose, Hazel, Ash, Birch, Rowan and Field Maple. There are excellent small waterfalls all the way along the Rookhope Burn.

Cross a footbridge over the tributary of Brandon Walls Cleugh. This walk along Rookhope Burn is quite delightful. Pass old mine workings, gradually decaying and blending in with the surroundings. Beyond the mines follow a track to a footbridge over the burn. Cross the bridge to reach the Rookhope road and turn left for 200m on the road, until a stile is found on the right just beyond a small wood. Go over the stile and head half-right

Turn right at the altar onto a minor road, following this to Holm House then carrying on a farm track to reach Hole House Farm. Walking along the road gives good views southwest, to the chimney and pipeline

towards   the wood fence line, but then slightly away before heading back again to the top of the wood. Cross the confluence of the small Deep Cleugh and Smail's Burn, to turn right and follow a wall on the right to pass through a gate into the farmyard of Smailsburn Farm. Walk through the farmyard and turn left and right to reach the back of the farm, and the old railway track. This was the Rookhope and Middlehope railway (a mineral line only) which opened in 1846 and ran from the north side of Weardale (stopping short of a junction with the main Weardale line) up to Rookhope. Here it joined the Weatherhill and Rookhope railway to run across Stanhope and Muggleswick Commons (with a branch to Stanhope) for about 21 km to join the main line at Parkhead Junction near Burnhill Station.

201

ROOKHOPE

Rookhope
Burn

473

Old Railway
Incline →

Smailsburn
Farm
Trees

Shafts

472

Ambling Gate
Bank

200

Turn right on the track and follow this all the way until just before Rookhope village, where a vehicle 'works' is reached. Drop right off the track down to the burn to cross the footbridge, alongside the old rail bridge, into the village. The line used to carry limestone and iron ore, and presumably lead. Just over the footbridge on the left, was the Weardale Lead Company. Rookhope used to be a very busy village with the railway taking out ore, but now is a quiet backwater.

Cross the road and head up a track to the left of Bolt's Burn. Beyond a few houses follow a left wall and when the wall reaches a corner turn left. Pass through a gate and walk on the track for 30m, turn right for 30m, then left to a gate at the right side of a wall. Turn half-right for 70m to a fence corner. Now head out across the moor in a northwest direction (330 degrees compass), to cross the east flank of Rimey Law. Because of its exposed position, applications have been made to erect a large windmill farm in the area.

D - E - O -
S LVANG
AVREINS
OVIRINVS
P - R 2 - Fo

Roman altar, Eastgate

Rookhope after a storm

The idea of wind-making power is admirable. However —

(i)   the visual impact is severe;
(ii) perhaps not always considered, the turbines make a great deal of noise as they are turned by the wind. This shatters the peaceful nature of the sites chosen for these enterprises;
(iii) an enormous number of windmills produce the same amount of power in a year as that produced by a normal power station in just a few days;
(iv) surely it is now environmentally acceptable, if this sort of environmental power is needed, to generate power at sea with the 'tidal duck' technology.

Lapwings and curlews keep you company as the route runs parallel to the valley of Stogel Cleugh (over to the right). Several false summits are passed on the way until the unmarked path reaches an unclassified road (Rookhope to Blanchland) at a height of 490m. The road is reached just to the left of a bend. Turn right on the road. Snow poles give a good indication of the sort of weather sometimes experienced. Walk on the road for some 200m, crossing over the beginnings of Stogel Cleugh at one point. 30m past the head of the cleugh is a signpost on the right marking a lead mining trail. Follow this distinct path once used by lead miners. Boltslaw Flat is to the left and Boltslaw West is to the right – both extensive moors.

Pass through a gate in a fence line and the path leads unerringly towards the cairn seen on Bolt's Law. The cairn can be seen for quite a distance. When Bolt's Law is finally reached there is in fact not only a cairn but a trig point marking the summit at

540m (exactly the same height as Abdon Burf in Shropshire, the highest point reached in volume one). There are

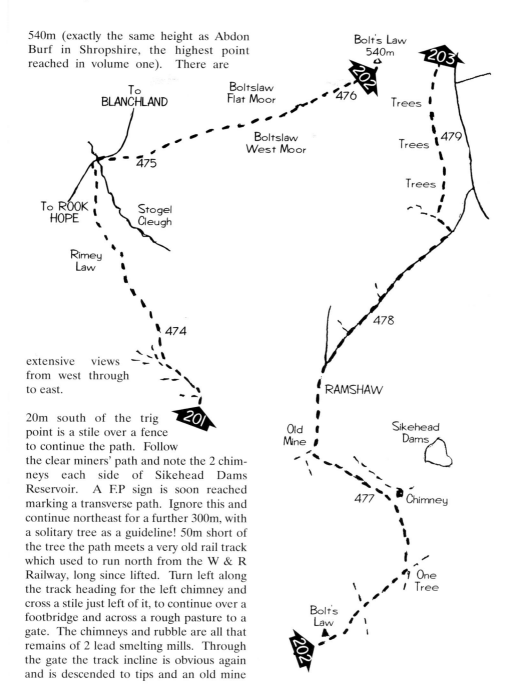

extensive views from west through to east.

20m south of the trig point is a stile over a fence to continue the path. Follow the clear miners' path and note the 2 chimneys each side of Sikehead Dams Reservoir. A F.P sign is soon reached marking a transverse path. Ignore this and continue northeast for a further 300m, with a solitary tree as a guideline! 50m short of the tree the path meets a very old rail track which used to run north from the W & R Railway, long since lifted. Turn left along the track heading for the left chimney and cross a stile just left of it, to continue over a footbridge and across a rough pasture to a gate. The chimneys and rubble are all that remains of 2 lead smelting mills. Through the gate the track incline is obvious again and is descended to tips and an old mine area. The scene here must have been quite something in the mining heyday.

Turn right on the mine access road. There are trees again! Bolt's Burn is to the right. There are also a few remains of a narrow gauge rail line. The mine track joins a farm track, coming from Boltshope Farm, to now have a proper tarmac surface. The road soon forks – take the right fork. Walk along the road and pass through the small hamlet of Ramshaw. The road crosses the burn and is followed for a further 900m until it bends fairly sharply left. 20m before this bend turn left on a track and pass

BLANCHLAND

GR NY 967 504

Abbey

204

River Derwent

480

203

through a gate. A barn is passed on the right and 50m beyond this the track is left by turning right along a wall side. The path goes through Deborah and Boltsburn Plantations for a pleasant woodland walk. At one point the path splits and the right path is followed on a higher terrace. The path eventually joins a woodland access drive. Turn right on this to reach a minor road.

Turn left on the road to descend Bale Hill. Just before reaching Bay Bridge (over the River Derwent), and opposite a road going left, turn right onto a woodland track. The track runs through the wood parallel to the river. Great Wood-rush is everywhere.

Blanchland Post Office

Another road is reached through a gate. Turn left across the beautiful bridge over the River Derwent and cross from County Durham into Northumberland, to enter Blanchland.

Blanchland is said by many to be the prettiest village in the whole of England, and who can argue? The name means 'White Land' and is named after the white robes worn by the Premonstratensian Monks who built the abbey here in 1165. Edward III stayed here in 1327 on his way to do battle with the Scots. After the dissolution of the abbeys in 1539 Blanchland Abbey became the property of the Radcliffes, then the Forsters. It was the Forsters who first used the abbot's lodging house as a manor house. Dorothy Forster married Lord Crewe (one of the Prince Bishops) in 1699 and he bought the entire estates in 1721. What was left of the old abbey was converted into the present church in 1752. The trustees of the estate carried out a complete restoration of the older village. The church has many remains of the abbey with medieval abbots' tombstones, an abbot's chair of 1550 and a 1500's embroidered altar cross. The abbot's

lodge became the 'Lord Crewe Arms' and must be one of the most unusual hotels in the country. There is a priests' hole inside the lounge fireplace, which was used to hide Dorothy Forster's nephew Thomas after the abortive Jacobite rebellion of 1715 (he was an army general for the Jacobites). The hotel has a number of bedrooms with an ancient theme. Quite the place to stay if you are looking for the exceptionally unusual, but also a good place to visit for a meal. Blanchland also has 'normal' places to spend a night such as the old doctor's surgery (still appropriately called 'The Surgery'). There is a medieval cross in the churchyard (with its shaft held in place by lead), which was originally a travellers' roadside shrine before being moved to its present site. The village houses were, in some cases, monks' living quarters. One of the houses in the square used to be a silver smelter's (silver is found in lead ore). More up to date, the village was used in 1995 for the making of the film *'Jude'*, from the novel *'Jude the Obscure'* written in 1895 by Thomas Hardy.

Medieval Cross, Blanchland

THIRTY FIVE
Blanchland - Allendale Town
(11.0 miles or 17.6 km)

Walk along the road going west from Blanchland to Baybridge. When the road turns left, leave it and go straight ahead on the private drive signed 'Newbiggin Hall'. Pass the Wesleyan Chapel on the right and arrive at the very large complex of Newbiggin Hall. Go through a gate and the tarmac changes to a stony track. Follow the farm drive as it bends right round the hall and passes

to enter High Beldon Plantation. The main block of trees is soon

BLANCHLAND
GR NY 967 504

481
BAYBRIDGE
River Derwent
Newbiggin
482
Long Plantation
204
205

ruined stables on the left. Follow the left wall along the edge of Long Plantation Wood. When the wood ends pass through a gate to continue following the track along a left wall. The wall ends but the track continues across a field

passed and the track goes along the right side of the plantation. The tree line bends left, but the track is followed as it continues ahead. Middle Plantation is passed over to the right as the track crosses Beldon Side, with

River Derwent bridge, Blanchland

Beldon Burn down to the left.

After 200m a milestone is reached, marked
R.I.M. At this point it becomes obvious
that the track was the ancient highway
going west from Blanchland to
Riddlehamhope, Harwood Shield and

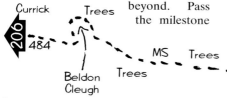

beyond. Pass
the milestone

and enter
Beldon End Plantation
(Scots Pine). The track descends to Beldon
Cleugh and the trees are left behind, before
climbing quickly to 354m and bearing
sharply right. There is a currick (not a
name to be found in the Oxford Concise
Dictionary) to the right. This is the old

Northumbrian word for what most people
know as a cairn. There are more curricks to
be seen to the south of the Beldon Burn
valley, and many more will be seen before
reaching Berwick.

The 'road' to give a better description
rather than track, ends at a stile giving
access to a small wood. The road continues
as a green track through the wood, to exit
via a gate at the abandoned
hamlet

of Riddlehamhope.
Follow the right wall, which soon bends
right around a stand of hardy Scots Pines,
to head north. Harwoodshield Fell is
crossed to another milestone and Espy
Sike. The road now has a tarmac surface

Beldon Side

and soon reaches the substantial Harwood Shield Farm.

Once the farm is reached turn left to follow a right side wall for 2 fields, then bear slight-

Rowan Tree Cleugh

486

ly right to follow a fence line (with sheep-fold to the right). At the fence corner leave the farm track to turn half-right and descend to Stobbylee Burn. Climb the grouse shooters' wide track on the other side, which now runs parallel to the deep

Stobb Cross

Currick

489

cleft made by the burn through Rowantree Cleugh. Cross Lilswood Moor on the wide track, which swings slightly left as the cleugh ends, to

drop down to the bridge over the junc-tion of Black Sike with Linn Burn. There are 2 exposed pipe lines here, and a wall! Turn half-left and follow the shooters' track along the left side of the wall for 400m. The track then bears left (just after a shelter hut), but the path goes straight ahead along the wall side. At this point a stand of trees some 2km ahead on Green Hill can be clearly seen, and acts as a guide for some distance (but the GEW path is going well north of the trees). Keep following the wall and eventually a currick on the height of Stobb Cross comes into view (at 400m). Carry on along the wall and descend (and climb) the depression of Knight's Cleugh. Wheatears should be

Knight's Cleugh

seen in the area. They are summer visitors, but usually arrive in April. The male has a grey crown and back with a black mask and white rump, with the female having a much browner back.

Keep along the wall until it turns sharp right, then head straight for the currick – crossing a signed transverse bridleway en route. The path runs to the left of the currick to reach a wall gate and farm fields again, as Allendale begins to show its beauty ahead. From this point a wide walled farm track is followed to meet a minor road. Turn right on the road for 30m,

Harwood Shield Farm

MS

485

Riddlehamhope

then left on the farm access track to High Scotch Hall Farm. Follow the track as it bears right beyond the farm, then go through a stile in the left wall and turn half-right to the far left field corner. Go over a stile and then slightly left to reach Finney Hill Green Farm. Pass in front of the farm-house then

Bridge & Pipelines

488

through a stile to head for the corner of a wood at Prospect Hill. Allendale Town is now spread out below. Follow the left wall through this field and the next to cross a farm track and stile. Over the stile turn

487

Blackett Level meets Philip Burn

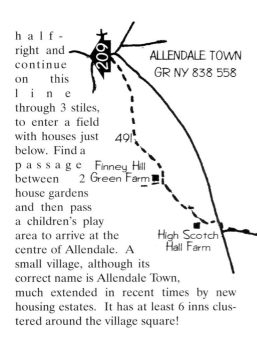

ALLENDALE TOWN
GR NY 838 558

h a l f -
right and
continue
on this
l i n e
through 3 stiles,
to enter a field
with houses just
below. Find a
p a s s a g e
between   2
house gardens
and then pass
a children's play
area to arrive at the
centre of Allendale. A
small village, although its
correct name is Allendale Town,
much extended in recent times by new
housing estates. It has at least 6 inns clus-
tered around the village square!

Allendale Town is the geographical centre
of Britain. The original village has small
cottages of brown sandstone built for and
by lead miners and quarrymen in the 19th
century. The village has a unique event
every New Year's Eve when the pre-
Christian 'Tar Barrel Ceremony' is enacted.
This is said to have taken place for the last
1500 years, where a large group of 'guisers'
(men) blacken their faces and carry barrels
of flaming tar on their heads (although
nowadays it is a mixture of wood shavings
and paraffin) around the village. There is a
bonfire in the square and a large crowd is
attracted to the proceedings.

THIRTY SIX
Allendale Town - Bardon Mill
(9.6 miles or 15.4 km)

From the village square take the B6295 road past the Allendale Inn and the Hare and Hounds Inn. 30m after the road turns left turn sharp right into a walled track leading down to

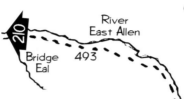

the River East Allen. Walk along the riverbank until a ruined building is reached. Alongside is a tunnel cut into the hillside, with a stream issuing forth. This is the Blackett Level, an ambitious scheme started in 1855 to cut a tunnel for 7 miles to Allenheads to drain water from the lead mines, enabling new lead veins to be worked. The tunnel was only completed for 4.5 miles before the industry collapsed, but still drains an enormous amount of water from the Allen valley. The level runs into the Philip Burn and then immediately into the river. Cross the burn by a footbridge. This is a very pleasant riverside walk to the road bridge of the B6295. At the road Catton is only 1km to the right with the remains of an old rail line even closer, which was the Hexham to Allendale line. Trains typically left Hexham at 0735, via Elrington, Langley and Staward to arrive at 0808. Running time was 33 minutes, with 30 minutes going back (one way must have been uphill!). There were 4 trains each day on Tuesday with 3 on other days. Hindsight is a wonderful thing. The line did not open until July 1922, so obviously was one of the last (and therefore least economic) lines to open. Sure enough, it did not make any

money and closed for passengers on the 22nd September 1930.

Cross the bridge and turn right on the riverside path. After 400m the path bears left through a small gate into a field and continues on the same line, only slightly further away from the river. Cross fields generally about 50m west of the riverside wall. Pass left of the fence surrounding the house at Bridge Eal. Cross the footbridge over Oakeydean Burn and continue to another footbridge over Crockton Burn and on to Kittygreen House. Go right of the house onto its drive, which is followed to Oakpool Farm and a minor road. Turn left and climb the road, then turn right on a farm track when the wood on the right ends. Follow the access track to Hindley Hill Farm. At the farm turn right through the farmyard and a gate to follow a left fence. Cross a small burn then turn right after 20m, crossing the middle of a field and skirting right of another burn, to cross a farm bridge over the River East Allen to Wide Eals Farm.

Pass left of the farm and onto its tarmac drive which is followed up to its junction with the A686 at a hairpin bend.

Turn partly right to walk up the steep road, choosing whichever verge offers most protection from the small amount of traffic. Down in the dale to the left the Rivers West and East Allen meet to form the River Allen. The road goes around 2 hairpin bends before finally reaching a junction (a strange elevated double junction with the road to Catton). Some 150m beyond this point turn left through a gate and head for the wood side across the field. Go through the stile at the end of the 1st field and in the 2nd aim right of the wall ahead, to reach the ruin of Gingle Pot Farm. Beyond this follow a wall on the right and when this ends carry on ahead, slightly left, to reach a gate into the wood ahead. DON'T go through the gate, but turn left to cross the field again to the wood lining the River Allen valley (Stawardpeel Wood). Find a stile leading to a path going down into the wood. The path drops through pleasant woodland to reach the river (ignore 2 paths going off left). Carry straight on through the mixed conifer and broad-leaved trees.

The River Allen in spate is a very very impressive river. There is a public right of way going north, but other permissive paths have also been provided. It is possible therefore to continue on a permissive path right alongside the river, to rejoin the right of way at a footbridge over Harsondale Burn and then continue along the riverbank. The River Allen is certainly the most impressive river on the GEW. Suddenly there is a gate with a field beyond. Leave the woodland path at this point to go through the gate and continue along the river. When a wall is reached keep to the riverside on a permissive path to arrive at Plankey Bridge. This is a wonderful suspension bridge, which evokes memories of some of those seen in the Indiana Jones films! Once across this bridge, which will give 'butterflies in the stomach' to many – go up a few steps and cross a footbridge over

211
River Allen
A686
496
To CATTON
River West Allen
495
Wide Eals Farm
River East Allen
Minor Road
Hindley Hill Farm
494
Oakpool
210
Bridge Eal

Farnalees Burn to a path junction. Turn left to climb through the 29 acre Briarwood Banks Nature Reserve. This is a classified 'Site of Special Scientific Interest', usually known by the acronym SSSI, belonging to the Northumberland Wildlife Trust. It is an 'ancient' natural woodland. Here you can f i n d (with luck) r e d squirrel, tree creeper and roe deer. The most common trees are Ash, Wych Elm, Sessile Oak, Birch and Yew. There is also an understory of Holly, Bird Cherry, Blackthorn, Honeysuckle, Hazel and Guelder Rose.

The path initially follows the burn side, but when it splits take the right fork going straight uphill. At the summit go through a gate to Briarwood Farm. Walk along the farm drive to reach a

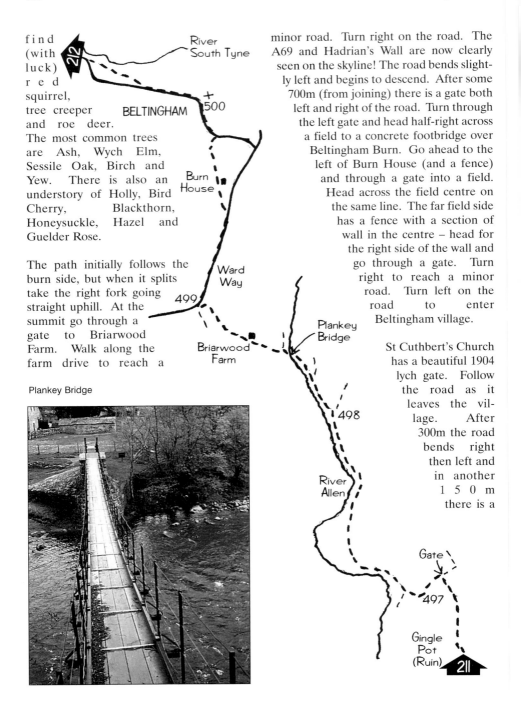

Plankey Bridge

minor road. Turn right on the road. The A69 and Hadrian's Wall are now clearly seen on the skyline! The road bends slightly left and begins to descend. After some 700m (from joining) there is a gate both left and right of the road. Turn through the left gate and head half-right across a field to a concrete footbridge over Beltingham Burn. Go ahead to the left of Burn House (and a fence) and through a gate into a field. Head across the field centre on the same line. The far field side has a fence with a section of wall in the centre – head for the right side of the wall and go through a gate. Turn right to reach a minor road. Turn left on the road to enter Beltingham village.

St Cuthbert's Church has a beautiful 1904 lych gate. Follow the road as it leaves the village. After 300m the road bends right then left and in another 1 5 0 m there is a

St Cuthbert's Church lych gate, Beltingham

stile on the right giving access into Beltingham Nature Reserve. There is a permissive path over the stile giving access to the route following the River South Tyne for Wildlife Trust members. (If not a trust member keep along the road). The route follows the river to rejoin the road at a bend. NB. This path through the reserve is subject to flooding, when the road becomes the only route!

BARDON MILL
GR NY 779 646

A69
Hotel
PO
213 501
FB
212
River South Tyne

When the road corner is reached walk along the road for 100m and turn right on the very long footbridge across the River South Tyne. Once on the north side of the river cross the railway (still working!) and soon reach the 'main road'. The original road is now bypassed to the north. Turn left to Bardon Mill.

Cottage at Beltingham

Looking back over Bardon Mill

THIRTY SEVEN
Bardon Mill - Wark
(13.6 miles or 21.8 km)

Bardon Mill is now a sleepy backwater since the bypass was built – and much better for this relief. From the 'main road' outside the Post Office enter the yard of Bardon Mill (now a pottery). Go through the yard, alongside the chimney, and walk straight ahead to a gate. On the far side of the gate is a track leading up to the A69. Cross with care and go left up the track opposite, through a gate and follow a right wall across a field, through another gate and onto the drive of Bankhead Farm. Turn left on the drive to reach a minor road. Turn right on the road to reach a road junction. Carry straight on (ie. the left road) uphill. Keep on this road for 250m until it bends left, where there is a stile in the right corner. Over the stile head across the centre of the field, turning left when the opposite fence is reached. Follow the fence with a wood and Chainley Burn to the right. The fence ends but there is a definite path to follow. A footbridge over Kingcairn Burn is crossed to reach Low Fogrigg Farm. Beyond this keep on a level running parallel to the burn. Keep to the left side of

Chainley Burn ignoring several footbridges offering a path to the right side. Vindolanda Fort suddenly comes into view! Follow the path by the burn to cross the footbridge (marked public right of way). A decision must now be made —

1. To carry on the path going to the right side of Vindolanda OR

2. To go through the gate and pay your entrance fee. There is no doubt that this must be the choice.

There are many gems to be seen in walking the GEW, and this is certainly one of them. Most visitors to the area in the past have probably visited the wall, or Housesteads Fort – which are very nice, but this is a reconstruction of a number of Roman buildings and is certainly a wonderful sight.

A little history must of necessity come next.

Claudius, Emperor of Rome, decided to invade Britain in AD43. Whilst the

Great Altars at Vindolanda

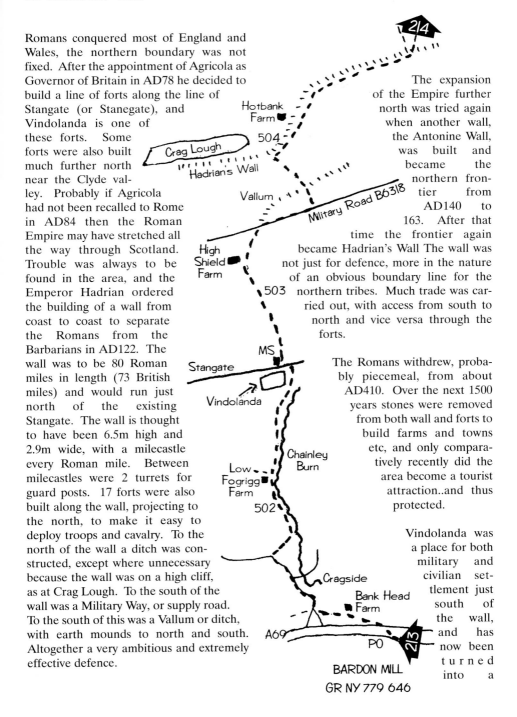

Romans conquered most of England and Wales, the northern boundary was not fixed. After the appointment of Agricola as Governor of Britain in AD78 he decided to build a line of forts along the line of Stangate (or Stanegate), and Vindolanda is one of these forts. Some forts were also built much further north near the Clyde valley. Probably if Agricola had not been recalled to Rome in AD84 then the Roman Empire may have stretched all the way through Scotland. Trouble was always to be found in the area, and the Emperor Hadrian ordered the building of a wall from coast to coast to separate the Romans from the Barbarians in AD122. The wall was to be 80 Roman miles in length (73 British miles) and would run just north of the existing Stangate. The wall is thought to have been 6.5m high and 2.9m wide, with a milecastle every Roman mile. Between milecastles were 2 turrets for guard posts. 17 forts were also built along the wall, projecting to the north, to make it easy to deploy troops and cavalry. To the north of the wall a ditch was constructed, except where unnecessary because the wall was on a high cliff, as at Crag Lough. To the south of the wall was a Military Way, or supply road. To the south of this was a Vallum or ditch, with earth mounds to north and south. Altogether a very ambitious and extremely effective defence.

The expansion of the Empire further north was tried again when another wall, the Antonine Wall, was built and became the northern frontier from AD140 to 163. After that time the frontier again became Hadrian's Wall The wall was not just for defence, more in the nature of an obvious boundary line for the northern tribes. Much trade was carried out, with access from south to north and vice versa through the forts.

The Romans withdrew, probably piecemeal, from about AD410. Over the next 1500 years stones were removed from both wall and forts to build farms and towns etc, and only comparatively recently did the area become a tourist attraction..and thus protected.

Vindolanda was a place for both military and civilian settlement just south of the wall, and has now been turned into a

Roman Temple at Vindolanda

showcase museum. There are full sized reconstructions of a Roman temple, shop, house and...a 1750 Northumbrian croft (complete with outside privy, or toilet). The museum is housed in the Chesterholm house and has a wonderful display of Roman writing, recently discovered, together with all sorts of everyday Roman artifacts. The museum also has one of those things loved by all walkers, a tea room.

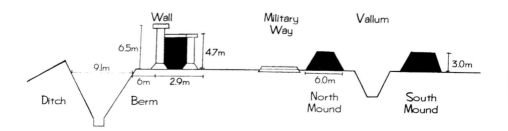

Wall Fortification...schematic

Hadrian's Wall

To drag yourselves away and continue on the GEW, walk out of the Chesterholm Museum on its access drive to the public road (or if you really could not afford the entrance fee, walk around the right side of the museum on the path to join the museum drive to the public road). Many people (who are not walkers) think that walking costs next to nothing, but those who are seasoned walkers know the opposite to be the case. The cost of Bed & Breakfast, together with an evening meal and a bit of shopping to put up your own lunch, over the period you have allotted to complete the walk comes to a great deal more money than flying off on a package holiday! Walking is a lot more beneficial to both body and soul, and look what you have done, seeing England in a way that none of the 'foreign holiday-makers' will ever achieve.

The public road now reached is the Roman Stangate. Turn left on Stangate for 100m then right over a stile. The Chesterhome Roman milestone is to the left. Climb the slope left of the wall and fence for 100m, then turn half-left up the field. Find a fence line and follow it to its left to reach High Shield Farm. Pass to the right of the farm, over a stile bearing right to reach the B6318 Military Road where the Roman Vallum (ditch) bends.

East Twice Brewed is just over 1km west, and Twice Brewed is 2km west on the road. There is a National Park Centre at Twice Brewed. The Military Road is nothing to do with the Romans, but was built by General Wade after the 1715 Jacobite rebellion to facilitate troop movements. Legend has it that the general visited the inn and not liking the beer had it brewed again, hence the name Twice Brewed!

Crag Lough from the Wall

BUT, the GEW turns right on the road, not left, for 400m – then left through a gate. The route now enters National Trust land. Walk on the farm track alongside Bradley Burn (which drains Crag Lough). The limit of established Roman Civilisation is reached...THE WALL.

Turn right on the public right of way alongside the wall. The GEW has now finally joined the Pennine Way, and will keep it company for the next 9 miles. Time to swop a few yarns with the PW walkers you will meet (who will have walked a mere 209 miles to this point, it's 504 miles on the GEW)

Crag Lough is to the left (lakes in England, lochs in Scotland and loughs in Ireland and ...here). Pass Hot Bank Farm and climb. There was a turret on the wall at Hotbank Crags (they all have numbers, this one was

37B, with a milecastle serving 2 intermediate turrets). After 0.5km descend to a dip, once the site of Turret 37A. At this point cross the wall (with Cuddy's Crags now to the right) and head diagonally right, initially aiming for the left side of Broomlee Lough. Cross a field, go over a stile and keep on the same line to pick up and follow a farm track. The track soon bears right, goes over a small ridge and reaches the walls of ruined Crag End Farm. Cross a stile, aim half-right then very soon left down a track. Greenlee Lough is now to the left. Cross a footbridge over a small feeder of the lough and turn right on a track. East Stonefolds Farm can now be seen. Cross a boggy area aiming for a point about 300m east of the farm, crossing a stile and footbridge en route over Haughtongreen Burn. Bear slightly left (away from the right wall) up a field to arrive at a wall level with, and 200m east of the farm. Cross the wall and turn half-right on a forest road to go through a gate and enter Wark Forest.

Of all the forests to be passed through from Hamsterley north-wards the Wark Forest is the easiest for route finding. For this we must thank Wainwright's Pennine Way. This being the first and most popular long distance route means that 'authorities' are aware, and therefore the route is very well sign-posted – and not plant-ed with trees – and if tree felling is taking place then an official diversion is well signed. It is 'a differ-ent kettle of fish' in the Harwood and other forests to the north, where paths are hardly considered!

The Wark is an irregu-larly shaped forest, some parts of which are traversed. For ease of reference therefore consider that 3 parts are to be walked through – the South, Central and East. Soon after entering the south part of the forest a path goes off right to Haughton Green, but ignore this and carry on forward on the forest road. The Pennine Way has been established for over 30 years and is well signed (some say over signed). PW signs are numerous along the

route, which means there is absolutely no problem in following this shared section between the PW/GEW. After a while the forest road is left and the route proceeds on a path, well signed. It is indeed a good job there are signs here since walk-ing a featureless path through fea-tureless conifers on each side is not easy! This southern section of the for-est ends at a fence where a stile is crossed into rough pasture land.

The ridge of Hawk Side is just to the south. The path crosses Sell Burn and a small walled plantation, to reach a stile into the central part of the forest. Again the path is well signed. 4 forest roads are met and crossed en route to the far side of this forest section. When the forest ends Ladyhill Farm can be seen ahead (to the right). A wall is met and followed on the left for the final stretch of trees and there are open fields beyond. Willowbog Farm now comes into view ahead. The wall is followed to a stile onto a minor road. Turn right on the road for about 300m, pass-ing entrances to both Willowbog and Ladyhill Farms. At the end of a wall on the left turn left off the road following a left wall for 300m to enter the eastern part of the forest. The wall ends at a new road which has been cut through to serve Stonehaugh leisure area and campsite 1km to the west.

The route crosses this road and then a forest road, where the path bears right to follow a broken wall. The final fence is reached and crossed to leave Wark Forest behind – a very easy passage.

Stride out across the field for 150m only, until the path splits at a marker post. The well worn path going half-left is the PW, but the GEW goes straight ahead on an undefined route through rough pasture. Head for the highest point of ground ahead which is Ground Rigg (241m). The top has a footpath marker post. There is a man-made embankment running west to east along the top, which is followed. Possibly a medieval turf wall? The embankment leads to Sadbury Hill farm. Go to the right of a barn, then bear left of the farmhouse onto the farm drive. What a change from the enclo-sure of the forest! This is now a vast open space.

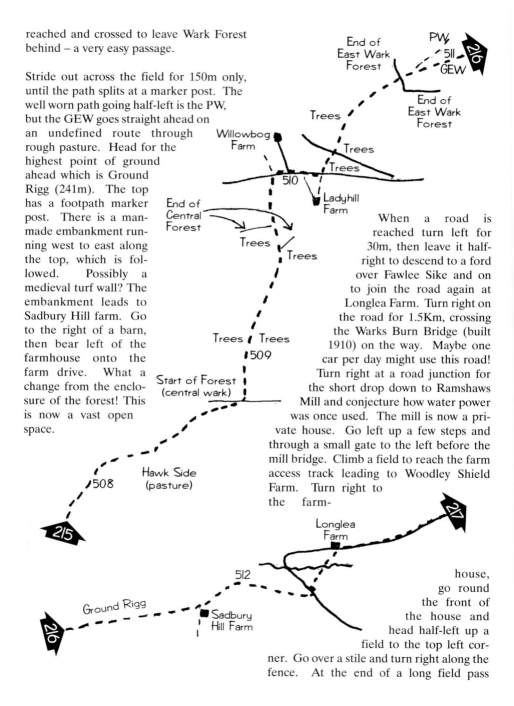

When a road is reached turn left for 30m, then leave it half-right to descend to a ford over Fawlee Sike and on to join the road again at Longlea Farm. Turn right on the road for 1.5Km, crossing the Warks Burn Bridge (built 1910) on the way. Maybe one car per day might use this road! Turn right at a road junction for the short drop down to Ramshaws Mill and conjecture how water power was once used. The mill is now a pri-vate house. Go left up a few steps and through a small gate to the left before the mill bridge. Climb a field to reach the farm access track leading to Woodley Shield Farm. Turn right to the farm-house, go round the front of the house and head half-left up a field to the top left cor-ner. Go over a stile and turn right along the fence. At the end of a long field pass through a small gate and continue along another right fence, through 2 fields, to a road. Bulbous Buttercup will be found along the path (one of 11 varieties of buttercup to be found in Great Britain). Turn right on the road to enter Wark.

The village is sometimes known as Wark-on-Tyne, since it

is situated at the side of the mighty River North Tyne. This is probably the site of the murder of Alfwald, King of Northumbria, in 788.

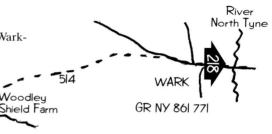

Approach to Wark

THIRTY EIGHT
Wark - Elsdon
(17.4 miles or 27.8 km)

Birtley War Memorial

Cross the bridge over the River North Tyne and turn left on the road to Birtley. The road soon crosses the bridge over the old railway. The line used to run from Hexham, via Wark, to Riccarton Junction. From that point there were connexions to Hawick, Carlisle and Edinburgh. Running time from Wark to Hexham was 28 mins and to Riccarton about 1hour 15mins. A road joins from the right and Allery Burn is crossed. Shortly after this pass through a gate on the left and then cross the field aiming for the left side of the wood on the horizon, to cut off the road bend. When the wood ends cross a footbridge and stile and climb contours. Birtley Castle used to stand here, but there is scant evidence on the ground. The path goes to the left of a house and garden and along a short passageway to reach the road opposite St Giles Church (founded in AD 1100).

Turn left on the road and pass the war memorial to enter Birtley. Pass the inn and carry on to the end of the village where the road bears left. Leave the road to go straight ahead to Townhead Farm. Just before the farm turn right through a gate and then left to walk behind the back of the farmhouse. Walk forward across 2 fields (crossing a broken hedge line after the 1st), about 100m away from the left fence. Cross Dinley Burn over a footbridge. Turn half-left for 100m and go through a gate. Strike out across the field centre to a stile onto a road. Turn right on the road for 10m, then take the left road at a fork for 20m, then over a stile at the right near a small wood corner. Turn half-left to cross an embank-

River North Tyne looking south

ment, then keep on this line heading for the right side of some scattered trees on the skyline. Soon a marker post and a trig point (249m) can be seen ahead at the summit of the beautifully named Rubbingstob Hill.

When the trig point and a minor road are reached turn right on the road. The views north and south from here

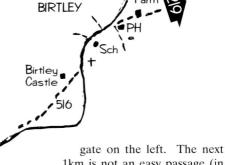

stretch well over 50 miles on a clear day. Walk along the road for 150m to reach a

gate on the left. The next 1km is not an easy passage (in 1997). Turn left through the gate to cross a field to the left side of a fence and arrive at the front door of Bog Shield Farm. Turn right and climb a fence. Next follow a left fence to meet a cross fence, which is crossed (no stile in 1997). Head up a field on the same line towards the ruin of Quarry House, crossing another fence on the way. When the wall before the house is reached, DON'T cross, but turn right along the wall-side. The wall changes to a fence and is followed to the field end and ruin of Tone Thrasher Farm. Turn left here through a gate and follow the right side of a fence. Tone Hall and grounds are over to the left. Curve right to the right side of the wooded parkland of the hall. Pass through 2 gates, turning left and walk along a farm track to the right of the park trees. Pass through a gate to the tarmac drive of Tone Hall. Turn right and follow the drive to the A68 road.

Tone Inn is at the side of the A68 road, which is the old Roman 'Dere Street'. Turn left on the road for 70m, then turn right to leave the road through a gate and along a farm road to Whiteside Farm. Pass through 2 gates through the farm and continue on the farm road beyond. When a corner of the left fence is reached bear slightly right to leave the road. Walk across rough pasture to arrive at a cross wall 100m right of the road. Find an old stile and cross the next field aiming for the middle of White House Farm.

Pass the farmhouse and turn left before a barn. Turn right through several gates to pick up a track on the far side of the farm (with a wall now to the right). When the wall and track end go through a gate and cross a field parallel to the fence line 30m over to the left. At the far field end are 2 gates. Go through the gate on the right into a 2nd field. Carry on straight ahead, but gradually leave the left fence to reach an opposite stile. Cross the stile and Reed Sike to enter Cranberry Moss. It is likely that Cranberries did grow here, since it is a native plant of the British uplands, but the entire area is being planted with a new 'forest' in 1997. Walk straight forward on what will become a forest trail. Take care. The forest trail swings northeast, but there is a marker post showing where to leave

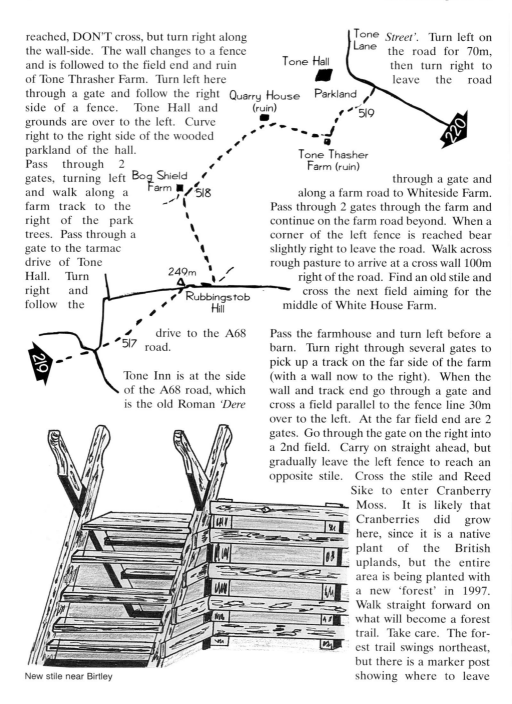

New stile near Birtley

the trail to continue east across rough pasture through the new trees. From this point it is approximately 400m (crossing Small Burn on the way) to a tall wall.

Don't cross the wall over the inviting stile, but turn left on a wide track. Follow this until it swings left, then leave it to continue along the

the left side trees end go through a small gate and continue along the wall. The flat top of Birney Hill is now to the left, but at least the vista has opened up again and

Sweethope Loughs are finally glimpsed. Keep following the wall to pass a barn on the left and pass through a gate into open pasture (the loughs can be visited by a path going off left just before the barn). Cross the infant River Wansbeck feeding the loughs. Turn half-right aiming for a 'bump' in the wall over to the right. Once the wall is reached (with Hawick Woods beyond), turn left and aim for the right side of a metal barn. Go through a gate and onto the tarmac drive of Hawick Farm which is followed north to a minor

wall side, aiming for a gate 50m left of the wall corner when it ends. Through the gate walk on a track uphill between trees to the left and a wall and trees to the right. When

'Over the garden wall', Whiteside Farm

road, passing Lunga Crags to the left on the way.

Turn right on the deserted road for 0.5Km, then turn left at a road junction (signed to 'West Woodburn'). The road bears right (with a small wood to the left) then left at the crossing of Middlerigg Burn. Just on the far burn side go right over a stile and cross a field, then go under the old railway bridge (which was the line from Wark to Riccarton Junction). Walk away from the old line but slightly left towards the fence at the side of the unnamed forest. This is not an easy point to find, but the fence climbs up from the southeast point of the forest for some 250m, then bends slightly – and there is a gate 150m right of this point.

Once the forest gate is entered the route goes along the same line as a forest fire break. After 250m a forest road is reached. Turn right on this 'road' which heads roughly north. The only landmark which can be seen from this area is the twin TV masts on Mount Gilbert some 4km to the north. Forest roads are for the commercial extraction of timber and do not necessarily go where you want to go! This is true in this case. After a while the forest road bears right. You now have a choice. The right of way goes ahead on a fire break (345 degrees compass). In 1997 this path was extremely difficult through a felled area, until finally breaking through to the original forest road and turning left. OR you can ignore the right of way and continue on the forest road which adds about 200m to the route, but ends up at the same place. Whichever route has

been taken the road goes almost to the end of the forest to cross a bridge at Threeburn Mouths. Just BEFORE this bridge turn right through a marked small gate. Cross the burn to follow the left fence for 200m to reach a separate small wood. This wood is lined by a wall which is followed north. The wood consists mainly of Scots Pine and Birch, which is a change from the unnatural non-native conifers.

When the wood and wall end go straight ahead aiming for the right side of the 2 buildings of Wishaw. A stone wall is seen ahead before the buildings are reached – go to the right corner and then follow a left wall to reach a fence level with the 2 houses.

Pass through the fence and climb to the right of the trees of Wishaw Plantation. Follow the fence lining the plantation and climb through the Heather of Whaup Moss. The going is hard through the Heather. The masts on Mount Gilbert have been out

222

Hawick
524   Wood

Barn ■

Sweethope
Loughs

523

Birney Hill   Trees
              Trees
       Trees
              Trees

Gate

222

Reed   Trees   522
Sike

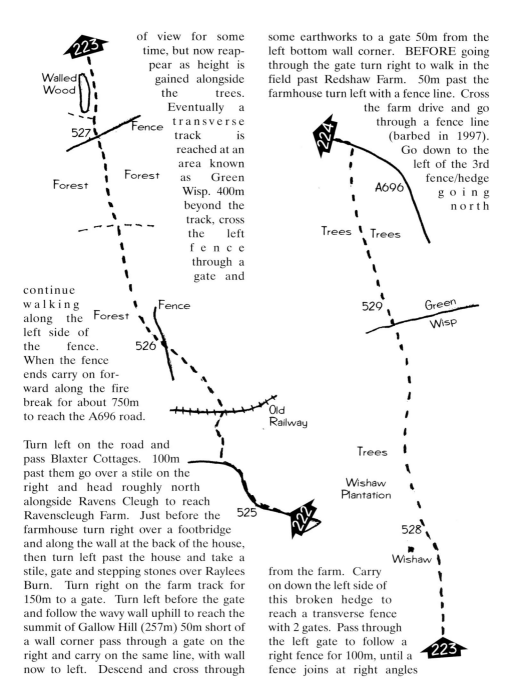

of view for some time, but now reappear as height is gained alongside the trees. Eventually a transverse track is reached at an area known as Green Wisp. 400m beyond the track, cross the left fence through a gate and continue walking along the left side of the fence. When the fence ends carry on forward along the fire break for about 750m to reach the A696 road.

Turn left on the road and pass Blaxter Cottages. 100m past them go over a stile on the right and head roughly north alongside Ravens Cleugh to reach Ravenscleugh Farm. Just before the farmhouse turn right over a footbridge and along the wall at the back of the house, then turn left past the house and take a stile, gate and stepping stones over Raylees Burn. Turn right on the farm track for 150m to a gate. Turn left before the gate and follow the wavy wall uphill to reach the summit of Gallow Hill (257m) 50m short of a wall corner pass through a gate on the right and carry on the same line, with wall now to left. Descend and cross through

some earthworks to a gate 50m from the left bottom wall corner. BEFORE going through the gate turn right to walk in the field past Redshaw Farm. 50m past the farmhouse turn left with a fence line. Cross the farm drive and go through a fence line (barbed in 1997). Go down to the left of the 3rd fence/hedge going north

from the farm. Carry on down the left side of this broken hedge to reach a transverse fence with 2 gates. Pass through the left gate to follow a right fence for 100m, until a fence joins at right angles

Walled Wood

223

527

Fence

Forest

Forest

Forest

Fence

526

Fence

Forest

Old Railway

525

222

224

A696

Trees   Trees

529   Green Wisp

Trees

Wishaw Plantation

528

Wishaw

223

from the other side. Turn right through the fence and go diagonally across a field down to a gate onto a road, which is joined just before the road bridge over Shaw Cleugh. Turn right to enter Elsdon village.

Elsdon has a large village green, with 14th century St Cuthbert's Church and its fortified parsonage (or pele) at one end. Professor Trevelyan wrote *'Elsdon remains today as the spiritual capital of the Middle Marches – the capital of Redesdale when neither Scotland nor England existed'*. Just north of the village is the Mote Hills with earth ramparts, which may have been pre Roman settlements. The hills later had a 1080 Norman motte and bailey castle.

William the Conqueror gave Robert de Umfraville the job of pacifying Redesdale. The family arms are still to be seen on the pele tower and inside the church. 1100 skulls have been uncovered near the church, which are thought to be the remains of men killed at the battle of Otterburn in 1388. Further afield (4km southeast on the Cambo road) is Winter's Gibbet. William Winter murdered Margaret Crozier in 1791 and was hanged at Newcastle. His body was exhibited at the spot now bearing his name. The name of Elsdon comes from *Elde* (meaning old) and *Dun* (meaning hillfort). The only inn now remaining is the 1781 'Bird in Bush Inn'.

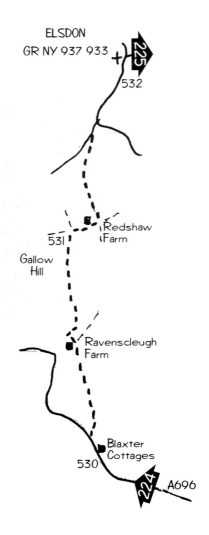

Traffic jam at Ravenscleugh Farm

River North Tyne

Cragside, Rothbury

THIRTY NINE

Elsdon - Rothbury
(14.0 miles or 22.4 km)

The section to Rothbury has its trials going through a long forest stretch, but is very rewarding before and beyond this area!

ELSDON
GR NY 937 933

Leave the village by passing St Cuthbert's Church. Cross the bridge over Mill Dean and turn right

follow it for 150m, then bear right to a foot-bridge over the burn. Bear half-left, then right to follow a fence up a field to the left of a small wood. When the trees end pass through a small wall gate to cross a field uphill to East Todholes Farm. Go to the right of the farmhouse, over a stile and turn left on the farm access road. Pass the front of the farm and follow a left wall, to go through a gate and enter Harwood Forest.

for 5m. A road goes left to toilets and Crown Farm, ignore this and go ahead through a gate and onto a tarmac road. Walk for 10m then turn half-right to follow a right wall/fence for 100m. When this ends go ahead along the flank of a hill to reach a wall corner. 10m right of this corner is a stile which is crossed to follow a left fence. Bend right, as the fence does, to almost reach Whiskershiel Burn. Turn right at the end of the fence to

Walk more or less parallel to the left wall through trees, crossing Mill Burn (a forest nature reserve area) to reach a minor road. Turn right on the road for about 1km to arrive at Whitlees Farm. There is no alternative but to turn right at the farm and delve into the forest. There is a signpost informing everyone that it is 1.5 miles to Manside. The forest is close and overpowering all the way! Head off along the path, to meet a forest road in 300m. Turn left on the road for 50m, then leave it diagonally left into a fire break at a marker post (opposite a small walled Scots Pine enclosure). There now follows an

View from Clennell Street

Ford Village

absolutely awful area of walking through tussocks of grass and Heather in a narrow area with dense conifers to each side. The only consolation we can think of is that it gives you time to ponder how wonderful other parts of the walk have been. A very straight trans-verse forest road is met, with a marker post. Go straight across and sometime later meet a very large forest road junction. Go straight across this also (marker post) on a slightly wider conifer avenue. The trees to the right suddenly end and the remains of Manside Cross lie forlornly in front. The base is intact but of the shaft little remains.

The area is now much more open, and the Simonside Hills can be seen to the north. There is also a fence line going eastwards, which is followed to its right. In 1997 much of this part of the forest

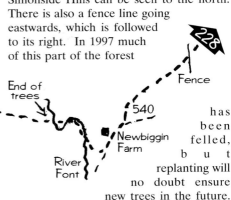

has been felled, but replanting will no doubt ensure new trees in the future. The fence leads to another major forest road junction. Carry on forward on this 'road' until it bends right after 200m. Leave the road at this point to follow another left

Manside Cross, Harwood Forest

fence in the same direction. The fence ends at a tarmac drive. At last the GEW turns north again. Follow the drive left to reach Redpath Farm. It takes a special kind of person to live in such a quiet solitary place such as this. Pass the farm and turn left off the drive and up to a stile access into the east part of the forest. Again a narrow conifer avenue is followed to arrive at a forest road*. The area north of here is being felled in 1997, and is in an awful mess. To follow the official path go through a 'door' in a deer fence and fight through a tangle of ripped up tree roots on a path marked with the occasional iron rod to reach another deer fence 'door'. Then go right to find a forest road in about 30m. Turn left to follow the road to Fallowlees Farm. OR* turn right on the forest road and follow it as it soon swings left and goes north to reach the farm.

From the farm the GEW goes east to leave the forest, then north over the Simonside Hills to Rothbury.

At the junction of paths before Fallowlees Farm walk past the front of the farmhouse and through gates. Cross a field and through a 2nd gate to go slightly right onto a forest track through the last part of this claustrophobic forest. There are 5 types of forest path – Heather, tussocks, bog, felled trees and 'level' grass. The last type is by far the best and is followed through this last section. When the trees end on the right go through a deer

gate, bearing half-right to a 2nd deer gate and the forest is finally left behind. Descend to a gate giving access to the River Font. There is no footbridge and you must ford as best possible. Turn half-right for 100m to cross the river

again, but this time with a footbridge. In a further 100m a small gate is passed through, then another footbridge crossed to the left. Turn right and gradually climb the left hill to a fence corner 150m right of Newbiggin Farm. At the corner turn left for 50m, then left over a stile to go to the top right corner of the field in front of the farmhouse.

Cross the stile and turn right along the farm road for 150m to pass a small field system on the left. Turn left at this point onto a farm track (with fence to left). After 70m on the track turn half-right to cross the field and then cross a fence 50m from the top left corner. Follow a left fence and when it bends left carry straight on to a gate 100m from the far left corner. Go through the gate to enter open moorland. Head straight on aiming for Blueburn Farm and its surrounding wood. Gradually aim right of the farm to reach a gate in a cross fence. Turn half-right to another fence, then left. At the field end, just past a barn, turn right through a gate and follow the right fence to a gate and the wood. Pass through the gate and walk in front of the farm. When the wood on the left ends turn left through a

g a t e . ROTHBURY
GR NU 057 017

Follow the fence to the right of the wood, then the fence which goes north from this point. Gradually head away from this fence by about 100m to find a footbridge across Blue Burn at the bottom of the field. This is followed after 20m by a footbridge over Spylaw Burn.

Turn left beyond the burn for 50m to a small gate, then turn half-right to climb diagonally away from a fence line (10 degrees compass) for almost 1km across a rough pasture. Just before Forest Burn (with which you have been converging) turns quite sharply left, go through a gate on the right and descend to a foot-bridge. Over the bridge turn half-left and pass a stone sheep-fold. Go through a fence

(map labels) 230 · 546 · Whitton Farm · Tower · WHITTON · 545 · Whitton Dean · Fort · Alternative Lordenshaw Estate Route · 544 · Car Park · GEW · Garleigh Hill · Lordenshaw Farm · 229 · River Coquet

gate and then ahead for 250m to a fence and stile. Cross and turn left for 300m alongside the fence to reach another stile on the left. Ignore this stile and signs to turn **right** and head away at right angles from the fence. In 800m the left side of Streethouse Plantation is reached. Pass alongside the wood and through a gate onto a minor road. Turn left on the road for 600m, then either—

A.   Turn right along the drive to Lordenshaws Farm. These are the Simonside Hills which give good views as high ground is gained. Pass the farm front and descend to Lordenshaw Burn. Go over a bridge, through a gate and turn left. Follow the left fence. Garleigh Hill (with trig point at 268m) is to the right. A cross fence is reached. Go through the gate on the left (marked with a tall pole) and head across Garleigh Moor on the same line (the fence carries on but goes away to the right). Cross a high point and pass through a gate. OR

B.   Carry on along the road for a further 400m and turn right into a National Park car park. Lordenshaws contains a wealth of archaeological remains. There are an Iron Age Hillfort, Bronze Age burial mounds and much more which are open to visitors by an agreement between Northumberland National Park, the tenant

Open stone cist at Lordenshaws

farmer and the landowner (the Duke of Northumberland). There is a waymarked path to the hillfort, then a waymarked permissive path going roughly northeast to the 'gate' at the end of option A.

From the gate go slightly right to cross a field to a stile at the junction of a fence and wall. Go straight downhill to cross Whitton Dean, followed by a stile and then uphill to the left of a fence. Pass through a gate and turn right on the unmade Hillhead Road. A static caravan site is passed to reach Whitton Tower (known as Sharp's Folly. This was erected by the Rev Dr Thomas Sharp, rector of Rothbury from 1720 to 1758, for the relief of unemployment amongst local stone masons, and also as an observatory. It is the oldest folly in the county). Reach a road junction and turn right. Walk on the road for 50m, then turn

Scots Pine at Cragside

left to Whitton Farm. Pass between the farm motel and stables to cross a stile into a field. Rothbury is now spread out below, with Cragside beyond the trees on the far valley side. Cross the field heading for the left of a wooden fence, then through a kissing gate to turn half-right. Walk down a steep road to cross the bridge over the River Coquet and into Rothbury.

Rothbury used to have a railway line, with a journey time of just over an hour from Morpeth. There were 4 trains per day (except Sunday when no trains ran). All Saints Church font pedestal consists of the base of the ancient Saxon cross of Rothbury dating from the 8th century.

A visit must be made to Cragside. The National Trust property is only 1 mile from the town centre on the B6341 Alnwick road (or better still take the path going east from the River Coquet bridge along the river to visit Thrum Mill, once a busy flour mill, and alongside the *'Thrum'* a river chasm. Follow the path to the B6344 road, then the path slightly right opposite to the B6341 road near the NT entrance). The mansion was designed by Richard Norman Shaw and built from 1863 for Sir William Armstrong (who became Lord Armstrong in 1897). Armstrong became the leading industrialist in the northeast, with the invention of the Armstrong breach loaded gun during the Crimean War. The demand from overseas for his armaments made the Elswick works (on Tyneside) the largest in the world.

Cragside was extended to 1700 acres (almost 700 hectares). 7,000,000 trees were planted on the surrounding moors, with 3 lakes being created to enhance the woodlands and provide power for hydro-electricity, which had been developed by Armstrong. The house was the first in the world to be lit by this method. Armstrong lived in the house for 40 years, and used it as both a personal home and as an attraction for business visitors. Visitors included both the Shah of Persia and the King of Siam, who had come to purchase armaments.

The visitor today can see the 'Power Circuit', including the Ram and Power Houses with hydraulic and hydro-electric machines. The house itself is beautiful, just one gem being stained glass windows by William Morris. The gardens and parkland are extensive. The property is open early April to late October daily except Mondays.

Lord and Lady Armstrong's Monument, Rothbury

FORTY
Rothbury - Uswayford
(19.5 miles or 31.2 km)

Rothbury to Wooler is a long distance without any shops (except Thropton), requiring careful thought. There is accommodation up to Alwinton, but nothing from there to Wooler except Uswayford.

Farm. Just before the farm turn right onto a walled green lane. The right wall ends but keep following the left wall to almost reach a wood, then turn left over a stile to cross 2 fields and reach Physic Lane (a green lane possibly named after the monks who ran a hospital, now disappeared, and who collected medicinal herbs along the lane). Turn left. When the track ends (and tarmac begins) turn right after 50m down a passageway for 100m to join a 'road'. Follow

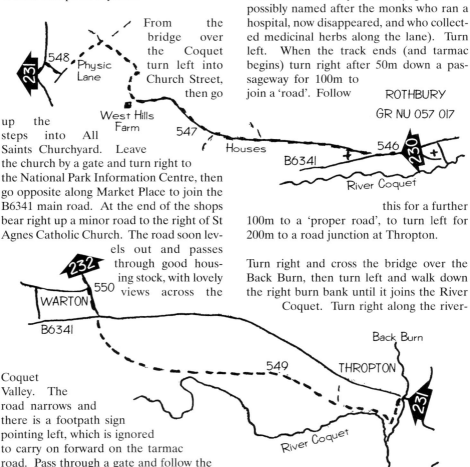

From the bridge over the Coquet turn left into Church Street, then go up the steps into All Saints Churchyard. Leave the church by a gate and turn right to the National Park Information Centre, then go opposite along Market Place to join the B6341 main road. At the end of the shops bear right up a minor road to the right of St Agnes Catholic Church. The road soon levels out and passes through good housing stock, with lovely views across the Coquet Valley. The road narrows and there is a footpath sign pointing left, which is ignored to carry on forward on the tarmac road. Pass through a gate and follow the road as it bends left, almost to West Hills

ROTHBURY
GR NU 057 017

this for a further 100m to a 'proper road', to turn left for 200m to a road junction at Thropton.

Turn right and cross the bridge over the Back Burn, then turn left and walk down the right burn bank until it joins the River Coquet. Turn right along the riverbank, pass a large foot-bridge and continue beyond this for 30m to a gate. Bear right (away from the river) and along a well defined path, with flood fields to the left. There is a beautiful smell of Gorse and Hawthorn blossom in the spring. The river is joined again momentarily at a meander, before the path continues along the left side of a field – then over a fence taking the path to the left side of the fence in a 2nd field. After 70m turn right over a stile to continue along the fence now to the left. Turn right on a farm track which is met near the end of the field to reach the B6341 road. Cross the road and go along the road opposite (signed to Warton).

After 250m the road turns left, carry straight on forward on a farm access track. When the left fence reaches a corner bear left

The track swings left then right around a small wood and passes the old Trewhitt Lake (now empty and overgrown). A minor road is reached. Turn right for 100m, then left through a gate. Head directly across Trewhitt Moor, aiming for the left of Sharperton Edge Plantation. Keep to high ground between burns en route. A fence line is seen and followed 100m to its south. Cross through a gate and gradually close with the plantation to follow alongside to a minor road. Turn left until Charity Hall Farm is reached. Opposite the farm entrance turn diagonally right to follow a

with it to aim for The Kennels Farm. Go through a small gate to reach the right of the farmhouse and a 2nd gate leading to a track behind the house. Follow the farm track with a fence to the left. Go through 2 adjacent gates to reach a bridge over Foxton Burn and pass through a gate to the left of a barn at Low Trewhitt Farm. Go through a 2nd gate and turn **left** in the farmyard. Follow a good farm track away from the farm to the left of a hedge/fence.

fence/hedge through 2 fields to arrive at the houses of North Sharperton. Turn left on the road to Sharperton (first written mention was in 1244 when Thomas of Sharperton was one of the jurors at Gilbert de Umfraville's death inquest) and a road junction. Turn right to cross the river bridge and carry on along the quiet road for a long walk to Harbottle village

To the right, just before the village houses, is a road leading to Harbottle Castle House (a 17th century mansion remodelled in 1829 by John Dobson in classic style). Just before its entrance and to the left, a path leads down to the River Coquet. Before leaving however the village has an inn and tea room. In 1160 the capital of Redesdale was moved, by the Umfravilles, from Elsdon to Harbottle and a motte and bailey castle was built. This was soon

235

Castle

Bridge

HARBOTTLE   556

River Coquet

replaced by a stone castle, where Margaret, wife of James IV of Scotland and daughter of Henry VII of England, gave birth in 1515 to a daughter (who became the mother of Lord Darnley, who fathered James VI of Scotland – later James I of the union of Scotland and

England). The castle is now a ruin and (at present) not open to the public. The last wolf in England is said to have been killed near here about 1750.

From the path to the Coquet cross the fine footbridge over the river. Turn left on the other side on a wide track. There are views of the ruined castle. Join a tarmac drive at Park House and reach 3

NORTH SHARPERTON

SHARPERTON

234

555

limekilns.   The practice of liming land in the county dates

Low Alwinton

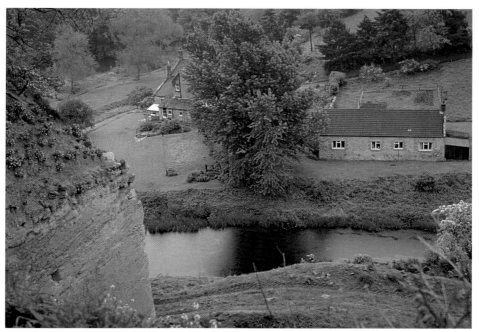

Heaton Mill House, River Till

Giant Hogweed

from the 17th century. Burnt lime was used to sweeten acid soil to produce better crops and improve rough pasture. Landowners built kilns mainly for their own use. These fine examples were built in 1827 and used until 1866. An information board explains how the kilns worked.

The road is joined at Low Alwinton. Turn right to pass the Church of St Michael and All Angels of Norman origin. Cross the bridge over the River Alwin to enter Alwinton and its 'frontier post atmosphere'. Sir Walter Scott wrote part of his *'Rob Roy'* in the Rose and Thistle Inn. Alwinton show is held every year on the 2nd Saturday in October and is the most famous in the Borders.

236

Castle Hills

Clennellstreet Farm

Fort

Hosedon Burn

ALWINTON

558

PH

River Alwin

LOW ALWINTON

Park House

River Coquet

557

Clennellstreet

235

Turn right to cross a footbridge over Hosedon Burn, then left onto Clennell Street. This is a prehistoric 'road' which ran from Alwinton, over the Cheviots, to Cocklawfoot some 19km away. Before railways, drovers would drive cattle over the border on the way to market in England (where they sold for more money). Clennell means *'Hills bare of trees'* and Street *'a road or path'*. The hills are certainly not bare of trees today, with the uniform Sitka Spruce plantations!

A stretch of tarmac is soon replaced by a wide stone track and a stiff climb is commenced. Castle Hills, with an ancient Briton hillfort built to defend Clennell Street, is soon passed to the left. Clennellstreet Farm is over to the

Lime kiln at Low Alwinton

right. The valley of Hosedon Burn opens up to the left with stupendous views all around (if it isn't raining or visibility is poor, which is not unusual in these parts!). The track is quite clear for most of its length. A fence gate is reached where the path splits. Go through a gate to keep following the

Ramparts & Royal Border Bridge

Berwick Town Hall (and finish point)

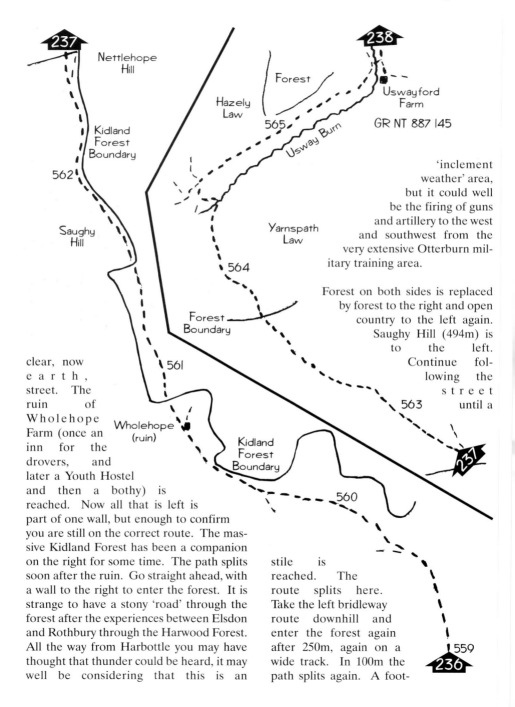

Nettlehope Hill

Forest

Hazely Law

Uswayford Farm

Kidland Forest Boundary

GR NT 887 145

565

Usway Burn

562

Saughy Hill

Yarnspath Law

564

'inclement weather' area, but it could well be the firing of guns and artillery to the west and southwest from the very extensive Otterburn military training area.

Forest Boundary

Forest on both sides is replaced by forest to the right and open country to the left again. Saughy Hill (494m) is to the left. Continue following the street

561

563   until a

Wholehope (ruin)

Kidland Forest Boundary

560

clear, now earth, street. The ruin of Wholehope Farm (once an inn for the drovers, and later a Youth Hostel and then a bothy) is reached. Now all that is left is part of one wall, but enough to confirm you are still on the correct route. The massive Kidland Forest has been a companion on the right for some time. The path splits soon after the ruin. Go straight ahead, with a wall to the right to enter the forest. It is strange to have a stony 'road' through the forest after the experiences between Elsdon and Rothbury through the Harwood Forest. All the way from Harbottle you may have thought that thunder could be heard, it may well be considering that this is an

stile is reached. The route splits here. Take the left bridleway route downhill and enter the forest again after 250m, again on a wide track. In 100m the path splits again. A foot-

559

Usway Burn

path goes off right into a very dark narrow gap in the trees – which is a path going to Uswayford via the north side of Yarnspath Law. Fortunately the GEW goes straight ahead on a clear bridleway going to the same place via the south side of Yarnspath Law! The street has a 100m wide avenue through the trees in this area, therefore that 'hemmed-in' feeling should not be felt.

The forest is finally left behind and the broad street becomes a path crossing rough pasture. A level is followed initially, but then the path starts to descend the contours of Yarnspath Law (if you really wanted to, on a clear day, you could climb to the summit at 543m to make this the 2nd highest point reached – yet). Usway Burn is reached and a waterfall. Cross a farm bridge, go through a gate and climb a field to a fence. This is crossed to turn right to a signpost* and then the flank of Hazely Law is followed, picking up the farm road to Uswayford Farm (built about 1800). This is one of the remotest farms in England and should you be staying overnight make sure you book well beforehand. *From this point you could climb to the ridge of the Cheviots in 1.6 miles (2.5Km), to join the Pennine Way, and follow this for 6.5 miles (10.4Km) to arrive at The Cheviot at 815m. BUT don't forget you would then have to return! Perhaps just too much after a long day, unless you wanted to make this into an extra day on the GEW.

FORTY ONE
Uswayford - Wooler
(17.9 miles or 28.6 km)

There is a footbridge over the Usway Burn to cross and get to its east side, north of Uswayford Farm, or you can walk along the right side of the burn from the farm if you have stayed there overnight. Either way walk north along the burn until you reach its confluence with the Clay Burn. Cross this burn and fol-

probably derived from the carriage of salt from the Tynemouth area over the border into Scotland. The road is quite well defined, with a wide path of grass unlike the Harwood Forest. A forest road is crossed and then the forest ends as open country is reached.

Salter's Road 567

239

Forest Boundary

566

Clay Burn

Usway Burn

238

Uswayford Farm

GR NY 887 145

low its left bank. There is a nice waterfall here, before entering forest area again via a stile. About 1km northeast from the joining of the burns the path joins the 'Salter's Road'. The 'road' is very old (a pre-historic crossing of the Cheviot Hills), but the present name is

The route becomes less defined, but keep walking easterly. Cross Foulstep Sike (wonderful names!). Don't lose height by following the sike, but keep heading east (actually ENE) to pass to the right of a large barn. The River Breamish is reached at the point where it is joined by the Ainsey Burn. A track is joined and the burn crossed before gates and a bridge take the path across the river. From here the GEW goes via High Cantle to reach Linhope (in bad weather, or if preferred, keep on the track which becomes wider and more or less follows the river to Linhope). There is an old railway wagon (they get everywhere) near

the bridge, go to the left of this and climb the field to a gate near the top right corner. Through the gate there is no path and you should make your way to the summit of High Cantle. The right of way goes about

Nagshead Knowe

568

High Cantle

Alternative Route

River Breamish

240

239

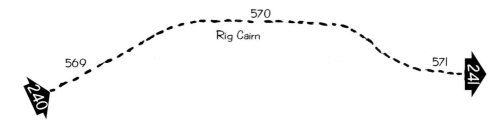

200m northwest of the 482m top. From the summit head for a junction of a broken fence and wall, then head roughly ENE through Heather without a path.   The object is to keep on high ground between the 'valleys' of the River Breamish to the south and Linhope Burn to the north. There are a few cairns (not curricks!) on the high ground.   When you begin to descend head for a fence/wall, beyond which is a vague track. The track becomes defined as it is followed to the west side of a wood to join a 'road'. Turn right and follow this downhill to pass a farm and cross a bridge over the Linhope Burn to arrive at the hamlet of Linhope. With time to spare a diversion can be made north along the woodside to reach the waterfall of Linhope Spout, which can be quite spectacular after heavy rain.

the top left field corner, then another gate giving access to a bridleway which leaves the farm track to head away across the base of Dunmoor Hill (the ancient village of Greaves Ash, long abandoned, but with some remains is to the left). The aim now is to head northeast (055 degrees compass) on a level contour, without gaining any height, until you arrive level with the end of Threestoneburn Wood (more a forest!).   At this point is another abandoned medieval village to the

right, but with little remains discernible on the ground. Turn north to reach a gate giving access into the corner of the Threestoneburn Wood.

Initially go through a gap between fence and trees for 200m, then on an ill defined path through the trees. The path goes not very far from the right side of the wood, but a forest is very thick and dark! Head roughly NNW (330 degrees compass), for about 800m where there is a gate in the forest fence to the right and a forest road is joined. Turn onto the 'road' and follow this north, passing over 2 small burns which join to the east to make the Harelaw Burn, for just under 1Km. When forest trails join

Leave Linhope on the road to Hartside and Ingram, after 200m leaving this left on a gravel farm track with a wood to the left, then through a gate and head for

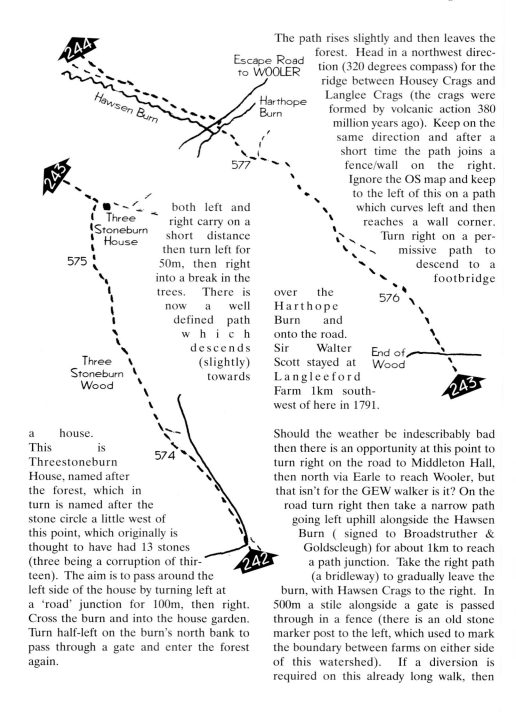

The path rises slightly and then leaves the forest. Head in a northwest direction (320 degrees compass) for the ridge between Housey Crags and Langlee Crags (the crags were formed by volcanic action 380 million years ago). Keep on the same direction and after a short time the path joins a fence/wall on the right. Ignore the OS map and keep to the left of this on a path which curves left and then reaches a wall corner. Turn right on a permissive path to descend to a footbridge over the Harthope Burn and onto the road. Sir Walter Scott stayed at Langleeford Farm 1km south-west of here in 1791.

both left and right carry on a short distance then turn left for 50m, then right into a break in the trees. There is now a well defined path which descends (slightly) towards

a house. This is Threestoneburn House, named after the forest, which in turn is named after the stone circle a little west of this point, which originally is thought to have had 13 stones (three being a corruption of thirteen). The aim is to pass around the left side of the house by turning left at a 'road' junction for 100m, then right. Cross the burn and into the house garden. Turn half-left on the burn's north bank to pass through a gate and enter the forest again.

Should the weather be indescribably bad then there is an opportunity at this point to turn right on the road to Middleton Hall, then north via Earle to reach Wooler, but that isn't for the GEW walker is it? On the road turn right then take a narrow path going left uphill alongside the Hawsen Burn (signed to Broadstruther & Goldscleugh) for about 1km to reach a path junction. Take the right path (a bridleway) to gradually leave the burn, with Hawsen Crags to the right. In 500m a stile alongside a gate is passed through in a fence (there is an old stone marker post to the left, which used to mark the boundary between farms on either side of this watershed). If a diversion is required on this already long walk, then

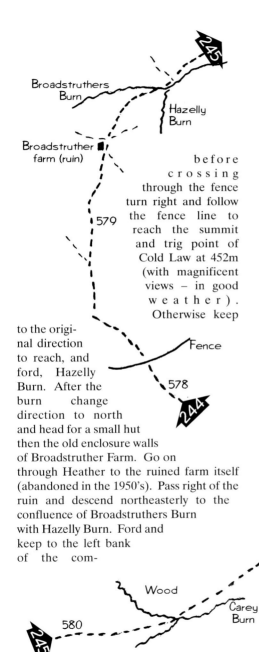

bined burn, until Common Burn comes in from the left. Cross a footbridge to continue alongside what is now Carey Burn, with an unnamed forest to the left. In 250m pass through a gate to the left and enter the forest. The path through the forest climbs and is known as *'Hellpath'* which is probably a corruption of 'Hill path'. The route is clear and the forest soon exited via another gate on a well defined path. Head for the left of a small plantation (with an ancient field system over to the left) and then pass through a gap as a 2nd plantation joins from the left. Follow a fence/derelict wall to the house of Wooler Common, turning left through a gate just before the house then a stile to turn around the house. Make for a fence to the right and then follow alongside (ignoring a track going off left up to a road).

The well defined route enters another forest (more a large wood) on the lower slopes of Earle Whin and ascends gradually, before reaching a point where it descends! Leave the forest and head across an open area of Gorse and turf for the left side of Waud House. Go along the house drive to reach Common Road. Turn right to walk to Wooler. The town marks the end of forests, thank goodness!

before crossing through the fence turn right and follow the fence line to reach the summit and trig point of Cold Law at 452m (with magnificent views – in good weather). Otherwise keep to the original direction to reach, and ford, Hazelly Burn. After the burn change direction to north and head for a small hut then the old enclosure walls of Broadstruther Farm. Go on through Heather to the ruined farm itself (abandoned in the 1950's). Pass right of the ruin and descend northeasterly to the confluence of Broadstruthers Burn with Hazelly Burn. Ford and keep to the left bank of the com-

Wooler has been spelt in several ways in the past (*Willora, Wollouer and Wolavere*), but they all seem to mean *'Stream Bank'*. William I gave the barony to Robert de Muschampe, and a market charter was granted in 1199. There was an early motte

and bailey castle, later rebuilt, but virtually
nothing now remains. Troops were stationed in the town for protection against
Scottish Reivers in the 16th century.
Daniel Defoe also probably stayed in the
town on his way to climb The Cheviot in
1728. A town trail leaflet is available
from the TIC giving more information
about the town and its history.

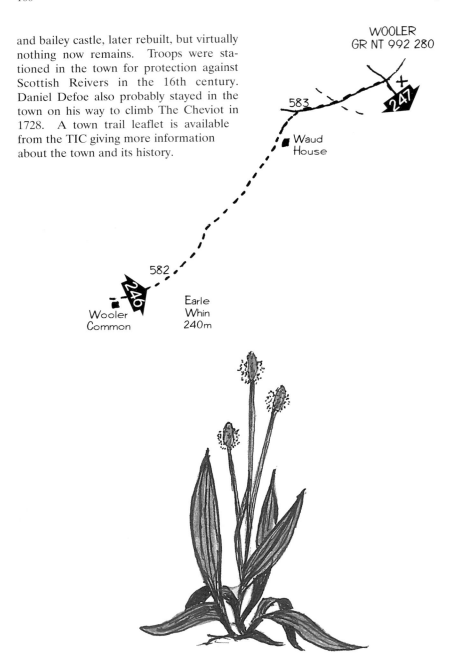

Ribwort Plantain *(Plantago lanceolata)*

FORTY TWO
Wooler - Ford
(11.9 miles or 19.0 km)

Leave Wooler by walking down Peth Head and The Peth (streets) to the A697 road. Cross the bridge over Wooler Water on South Road and go straight across onto Brewery Road. Pass the Brewery Inn to the left and Haven caravan site right (on the site of the old rail line). The road begins to climb, then bends half-left for 100m, (then right to the radio transmitters). Leave the road on the left at this point (signed to Weetwood Moor, and also St Cuthbert's Way). Pass through 2 gates and start climbing diagonally right up to Weetwood Moor, going away from the left fence. There are many paths across this moor. Keep straight ahead on the signposted St Cuthbert's Way (this is the 100km route linking places associated with St Cuthbert and running

wood and turn left to descend across a field. Go to the right of another small plantation, then through a gate and descend diagonally right towards Weetwood Bridge, with a final stile just west of the bridge onto the B6348 road.

The 16th century Weetwood Bridge was used by the English army on its way to the Battle of Flodden. Cross the bridge

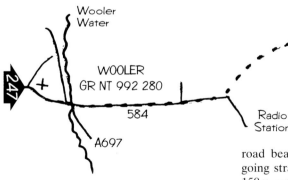

from Melrose to the Holy Island), ignoring all other paths to finally reach an area of tumbledown walls. The OS map and reality on the ground now differ, the best route seems to be – pass through a gate to carry on now with a fence to the left, aiming for the right side of a small wood. Pass the

(now restricted for weight to save further damage) over the River Till. Walk along the road, passing a road junction going off left. Shortly after this the road bears right, leave the road here by going straight ahead on a narrow lane for 150m until the lane turns left. Carry straight on a green lane signposted to Doddington. The Green Alkanet, with its beautiful blue flowers, grows in profusion along the lane. Pass a small copse on the right and the green lane ends at a gate. Continue uphill following a right fence. Struggle on, this really is the last hill to be

Weetwood Bridge over the River Till

climbed on the GEW!. Go over a stile to the right of a tumbledown wall and follow an old wall to the left. When this ends strike out across a field on the same line, to gradually come closer to the wall on the right (and a small plantation beyond). When the trees end carry on for a further 150m (with cup and ring marked rocks over

Weetwood Bridge over River Till

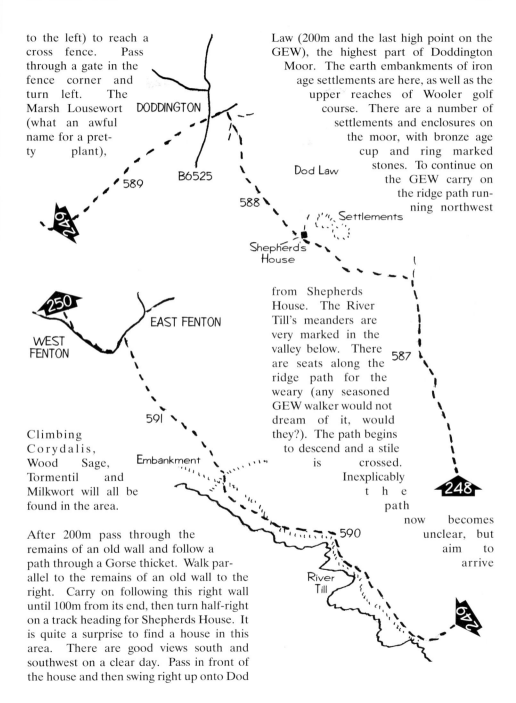

to the left) to reach a cross fence. Pass through a gate in the fence corner and turn left. The Marsh Lousewort (what an awful name for a pretty plant),

589

DODDINGTON

B6525

Law (200m and the last high point on the GEW), the highest part of Doddington Moor. The earth embankments of iron age settlements are here, as well as the upper reaches of Wooler golf course. There are a number of settlements and enclosures on the moor, with bronze age cup and ring marked stones. To continue on the GEW carry on the ridge path running northwest

Dod Law

588

Settlements

Shepherd's House

WEST FENTON

EAST FENTON

591

Climbing Corydalis, Wood Sage, Tormentil and Milkwort will all be found in the area.

Embankment

587

from Shepherds House. The River Till's meanders are very marked in the valley below. There are seats along the ridge path for the weary (any seasoned GEW walker would not dream of it, would they?). The path begins to descend and a stile is crossed. Inexplicably the path now becomes unclear, but aim to arrive

590

River Till

After 200m pass through the remains of an old wall and follow a path through a Gorse thicket. Walk parallel to the remains of an old wall to the right. Carry on following this right wall until 100m from its end, then turn half-right on a track heading for Shepherds House. It is quite a surprise to find a house in this area. There are good views south and southwest on a clear day. Pass in front of the house and then swing right up onto Dod

at a stile onto a lane to the right of a bungalow. Turn left on the lane to the main B6525 road at Doddington.

To the right is the cross topped well. Water used to issue forth from the spouts until 1957, when the river flooded and affected the water course and it has been dry ever since. Not far to the northwest is Doddington Bastle (a building more ambitious than a simple Pele) built for the Grey family. It was built in 1584 just as the border troubles were in a quiet period, and therefore was built for a residence as well as defence. It was a thick stone-walled 3 storey house but is now a ruin. The churchyard has an early 19th century watch-house, built to guard against bodysnatchers from Scotland.

The area now entered is known as the Millfield Plain, which was a vast lake when the glaciers melted from the Cheviots. Turn left on the road for 20m then right down a lane. When the lane swings right carry straight ahead on a wide track (signed to Bridge End). The north end of the Cheviot range fills the sky ahead. The River Till and bridge are reached. The Till is the only English tributary of the mighty Tweed. From this point until the hamlet of Fordhill the paths are in need of attention in 1997, but walkable. At the bridge turn right then left (through a sheep pen) to follow the left fence and flood embankment. There are 4 fields to negotiate to reach a junction of embankments. In the 1st field initially follow the embankment on the left, then where the embankment bears left go straight ahead to cross a fence (aiming for the embankment where it turns back from the river). In the 2nd field, having regained the embankment, follow it to a gate. In the 3rd field follow the embankment as it bears

Cup and Ring marked stones near Dod Law

left, then cut the corner to rejoin it at the fence at GR NT 947 377 the end of the field. In the 4th field go through a gate on the left after 100m to cross to the river side of the embankment, then swing right to rejoin it at the field end. There are 2/3 barbed wire fences to negotiate to cross an unnamed tributary feeder (perhaps better to keep on the top of the embankment to cross the feeder until the situation has been resolved). Beyond this point cross a field diagonally right to reach a fence line, which is followed to reach a cross fence. Go through the fence into an open field, crossing it aiming for the buildings between West and East Fenton. A hidden fence is crossed part way, with an old stile. Finally a wall is reached with a barbed off stile and a signpost!.

Fenton used to have its own tower, built in 1415 and extensively

repaired in 1542. Sir John Forster commanded 100 men here in 1549. Sadly there are no remains now left of the tower.

Turn left on the road, bending right with it, as it passes West Fenton Farm. After approximately 400m the road bears sharply left, at this point turn

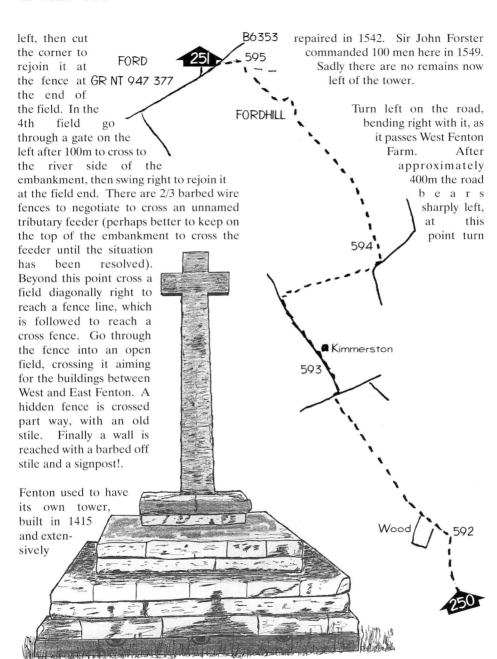

FORD

B6353

251

595

FORDHILL

594

593

Kimmerston

Wood

592

250

Water cross at Doddington

half-right onto a green lane. The lane climbs, then bends sharp left to an unnamed plantation, becoming an obvious farm access track. At the end of the plantation the track carries on for a further 250m to pass through a fence line, then climbs slightly across the next field and ends. Cross a fence (no stile) and head directly across the next field to reach a road at a gate. Turn right for 50m on the road to a T junction and turn left along another minor road, which passes Kimmerston Riding Centre. The road crosses West Kimmerston Bridge over the Bradford Burn. Beyond the bridge pass 1 field on the right, then turn right through a gate and follow the left side of a hedge/fence. Eventually a fence comes in from the left and in a further 100m the right fence bends sharply right. Strike straight ahead for 200m to a gate onto a road at a bend. Go ahead on the same line along the road for 200m to a sign and stile on the left. Over the stile head out across the field at right angles to the road to cross one field to a broken fence stile. Cross the next field aiming for the right side of a line of Hawthorn trees, to go through a gate and onto a farm track. Pass through more gates along the track until one final gate where the track turns right.

Take the 2nd track to the left to pass through Fordhill. This was originally one large farm, but is now a hamlet with several houses as well as a farm. Aim for a line of terraced bungalows and turn left in front of No 1. This is a very nice but most unusual complex. After 100m turn right through a gate to follow a left hedge uphill. Pass through a gate and steps into Fordhill Wood. 20m after the steps cross a broad track and go ahead on a path through the wood, which leads down to the B6353 road.

The old smithy at Ford

Turn left then right at the 2nd turn to enter Ford village.

This is a 'Model Village' with a lot of history. The first house was built on the site by Odinel de Ford in the 13th century. It was turned into a castle by William Heron in 1338 and was taken by the Scots in 1385 and dismantled. It was rebuilt about 1509 only to be taken again by James IV of Scotland, who spent a few nights here (before his defeat at Flodden Field in 1513), the castle was set on fire on leaving. By 1541 it had been partially restored, but was again attacked, this time by the French fighting for the Scots who wrecked what was left. The remains were turned into what is seen today by rebuilding in 1761 and in 1828. The castle had passed into ownership of the Marquis of Waterford in 1822. His wife, Lady Waterford, restored and rebuilt it in 1861 to give the present day castle (now a field centre).

Lady Louisa Waterford and her husband lived in Ireland, but she moved to Ford in 1859 after he died and began to rebuild the village. To her we must give thanks for the present day Horseshoe Forge (now a pottery), the marble Angel Fountain, the Jubilee Cottage and the Lady Waterford Hall (with a room decorated by water colour frescoes painted by Lady Waterford between 1861 and 1882). The well which used to supply the village with water is also still preserved. John Ruskin and Augustus Hare, as well as members of the Royal Family were visitors at the castle. The Joicey family bought the Ford and Etal estates in 1907, and added to the distinct houses in the village. The inn was closed in 1873 because Lady Waterford supported the temperance movement, but there is an inn at Etal.

FORTY THREE
Ford - Norham
(13.2 miles or 21.1 km)

To leave Ford pass by Jubilee Cottage and the Horseshoe Forge. Ignore a sign on the left signed Hay Farm and carry on down the road to pass the Ford and Etal Estate offices. In 50m (where the road turns right) turn left (signed Hay Farm) into Ford Wood. Cross a footbridge and exit the wood over a stile. Note;..there are permissive paths going left near the footbridge for an extensive walk around this delightful wood. Turn left from the stile along the wood edge for 100m, then turn right in the field to follow a left hedge. At the top of the field turn left, through a gate, to Hay Farm (part of the Ford estate, owned by Lord Joicey). This is another hamlet farm.

Turn right before the barns to reach a minor road. Turn right on the road for 50m, then left through a gate to follow a left fence for 100m. Turn right to follow a left fence to reach Shipton Dean Wood on the left. When the wood sweeps round to the right go through a left gate and over a footbridge to pass through the wood. On the north side of the wood footpaths have been altered from the OS map. Turn left along the wood side, with marker posts, for 200m. At the field corner turn right to follow the left fence and wood. The path soon becomes a farm track and passes a timber mill to the right to reach a road. This is the hamlet of Etal Rhodes and opposite is the

The Black Bull, Etal

Errol Hut Smithy. Turn left on the road and pass the ornate entrance gates to Lord Joicey's Etal Manor built in 1748. Join the B6354 road and turn right to walk along the pavement to Etal village. Turn left to the village centre.

Etal, Ford and Blanchland must be the most beautiful villages in Northumberland. Etal village was laid out in its present form in the late 19th century, but with additions in the early part of the 20th century. There is a quoits green. The Black Bull is Northumberland's only thatched inn. Continue down the only street to Etal Castle.

The house was crenellated in 1341, by the Manners family, to become Etal Castle. The castle was invaded by James IV at the same time as Ford Castle in 1513. Although not destroyed it slowly decayed after this time. The castle is now owned by English Heritage and is open to the public from 1st April until the end of October. There is an exhibition about border warfare and the Battle of Flodden in particular. The battle was fought near the village of

Branxton (4.5km as the crow flies from Etal). There have been many stories and poems written about the decisive battle – In 1513, just after the battle, John Skelton wrote *"Ballade of the Scottysshe Kynge"* and in 1808 Sir Walter Scott wrote *"Marmion, a tale of Flodden Field"*.

Outside the castle are 2 cannons, which came from 'The Royal George' a warship which sank near Spithead in 1782 with the loss of 300 lives. At the rear of the castle is a 15 inch gauge steam rail line which runs from here to Heatherslaw (40 mins return time) to visit Heatherslaw Corn Mill, a restored 19th century water-powered corn mill (with gift shop and tea rooms).

To continue the GEW follow the road down to the River Till. Some 50m before the river is reached turn right to walk up above the river bank. From here to Berwick will be mainly delightful riverside walking. The path is clear as it follows the river. A footbridge is crossed over Duddomill Burn and the path climbs slightly to a gate. Through the gate climb the field to a gate part way between barns to the left and Tindal House to the right. Turn right beyond the gate on a farm access track. Pass the house and a large dog pen

Map labels:
252, Dog Pound, Tindal House, Barn, 599, River Till, 598, Etal Manor, ETAL, Castle, ETAL RHODES, Smithy, Timber Mill, Diverted Path, FB, 596, Hay Farm, FB, FORD GR NT 947 377, 251

on the right, then after 200m more the track swings right. At this point carry on ahead walking to the right of a hedge. There are very large fields in this part of the county, with many hedges having been removed. At the end of the first field there is a fence junction. Cross the fence and bear slightly right to keep following the fence on the left. At the end of the next very large field join a farm track and turn left to Tiptoe Farm. This is another hamlet. Just before the farm is reached 2 tracks go left, one is earth and the other tarmac. Turn down the 1st (earth) track and then turn right near the river bank

onto a riverside path again. The path is now wide through broad-leaved trees. Castle Heaton Farm is on the other side of the river. The ruins of the castle cannot be seen from this side of the river. The castle history is vague, but it was built sometime prior to 1513 since the Scots raided and destroyed it in that year.

The path soon swings right on a diversion caused by a cliff landslide, which means the path now breaks out at the top of the riverside trees. A sign points left taking the path well above the river with a fence now to the right, to give marvellous views down to the Till and Heaton Mill House and crags below. This section is a lovely walk through Tiptoe Wood high up on the top of crags. All too soon the path descends through a field to the riverside again. A farm track is joined for a few metres but soon left to join the riverbank. After a while the path climbs up to pass the old Twizel Mill (now a private

253
602
Heaton Mill House
TIPTOE
601
Castle Heaton Farm
600
River Till
252

Etal Castle

Twizel Bridge

house). From here the house drive is followed to its junction with the A698 road.
The old Twizel Bridge with its single 90 foot
arch is now bypassed by a modern bridge,
but has been restored and is very beautiful.
The Scottish army are said to have marched
over   the
bridge   in
1513 on

the way to attack Norham Castle.

Cross the modern road to enter the gates of
Tillmouth Park estate. There are immediately 2 paths tempting the walker. The left
one is the GEW, but you can go straight
ahead to visit the ruined Twizel Castle first.
400m brings the path to the ruined castle,
often described as a folly. The castle dates
from before 1415, but was destroyed
in a raid by James IV in 1496
and not restored.   The
remains   were

River Tweed 254
605
Twizell
Castle
Twizell
Bridge
604
A698
603
Twizell
Mill
River
Till 253

incorporated into a new house begun in 1770, but after 48 years the building was stopped before completion, hence the 'folly'. On returning to the GEW continue along the riverbank. From here there is a stretch of some 8 miles (13 km) where a new plant has taken over from the native plant species – The Giant Hogweed (Heracleum mantegazzianum). The plant is an introduction from Southwest Asia. The leaves grow up to about 1 to 1.5m and are very deeply lobed. The flower stem can grow to 5.5m (18 feet). **Don't touch** because the sap can be caustic and cause burns and other problems. There are some warning signs, but you have been warned!

Fortunately there is a wide path cut through the Giant Hogweed and this is followed to pass under the magnificent railway viaduct. The line is now sadly lifted, but used to run from Berwick to Kelso (with a branch to Wooler and beyond). The train stopped at Tweedmouth, Velvet Hall, Norham, Twizell, Coldstream, and on to Kelso. The journey time to Twizell from Berwick was 27 mins, with 21 mins to

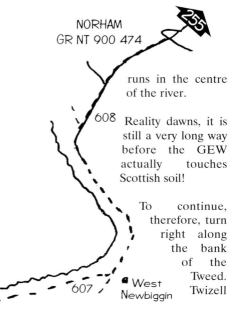

NORHAM
GR NT 900 474

608

607   West
       Newbiggin

606

River Tweed

254

Norham. It will take a little longer to complete the walk! Beyond the viaduct the ruins of St Cuthbert's Chapel come into view on the other bank. Suddenly the River Till joins the River Tweed. This is a very quiet and placid joining in a very quiet and placid spot. There is a seat on which to contemplate what has been achieved. The boundary between England and Scotland

runs in the centre of the river.

Reality dawns, it is still a very long way before the GEW actually touches Scottish soil!

To continue, therefore, turn right along the bank of the Tweed. Twizell Boathouse is soon reached and a track joined for a short time before becoming a path again. Milne Graden House and garden in Scotland look very attractive. Soon an island is reached. In fact there are 2 islands. The first one – Dreeper – is English. The second one – Kippie – is Scottish. The walk along the River Tweed can only be described as quite majestic.

The path climbs well above the river, then descends again. The islands end and the full width of the Tweed can be seen again. There are a number of fishermens' huts along the river confirming its good fish potential. The path eventually reaches an area below West Newbiggin Farm. Cross a footbridge and climb steps to a path meeting point. Turn left to keep alongside the riverbank through the Giant Hogweed. There is a 2nd magnificent viaduct (on the Berwick to Kelso line) to the right crossing the Newbiggin Dean. The path reaches a gate into a tarmac lane. Follow the lane, which soon turns right to Norham village (pronounced 'Norrum').

A motte and bailey castle was built here in 1121. It was taken in 1136 by King David of Scotland, thus the English/Scottish troubles were very long lived. The area was retaken by the English in 1157 and the castle rebuilt in stone in 1158. Norham was part of the County Palatine of Durham until 1844 (along with Holy Island and the Farne Islands). The keep built by Bishop Hugh de Pulset dominates the ruined castle. In 1318 the castle withstood a year long siege by Robert the Bruce and in 1319 the events occurred which led to the heroism of the Knight Sir William Marmion. This story was immortalized in the opening scenes of 'Marmion', Sir Walter Scott's long poem, written in 1808, about the Battle of Flodden.

Norham was attacked in 1513 in the fateful invasion by King James IV. The castle was put into ruins by the mighty cannon known as 'Mons Meg'. The castle is now owned by English Heritage and well worth a visit.

The village green has a market cross with a medieval 13th century base constructed from witches stones of a pre-Christian era and probably surmounted by a pagan symbol originally. Today the upper part is a sandstone quartefoil shaft erected in 1879, with a fish as a weather vane, showing how dependent the village was on salmon fishing. St Cuthbert's Church was built by the Bishop of Lindisfarne in AD 830. It was destroyed by David King of Scotland in 1138 and replaced by a Norman church in 1160. The rail line opened in 1849 and closed in 1965, but.the old railway station has not been ripped down. It is now a museum with a working signal box, model railway and collection of railway artefacts and Victoriana.

Norham Castle

FORTY FOUR
Norham - Berwick-upon-Tweed
(9.5 miles or 15.2 km)

Walk along Castle Street towards the castle. Before the road bends turn left into North Lane and immediately right, through a gate, into a picnic area and down to the riverside. Walk alongside the massive rock supporting the castle. Some 300m past the castle rock go over a footbridge and the path splits. Go right (uphill away from the river) to gain a path at the top of the tree line. Over a stile turn left along a fence above the trees. This is another area of very large fields. The trees begin to bear right at Red Rock outcrop.

About 100m before the end of the tree line go over a left stile to continue through the last few trees, through 2 stiles, to regain the right side of a fence in a field again. Cross a fence and change to the left side of a fence, to walk through another field and cross a stile onto a

farm access track. Cross the track and a stile and aim to go across the next field almost at right angles to the track. There is a marker post in the opposite hedge! Strike out on the same line across the next field, to reach a diagonal hedge coming in from the left. When the hedge/fence is reached turn right along it. Over to the left are the earthworks of an Ancient Briton Hillfort. At the end of the field go over a stile and turn half-left for 50m, then right to go round some sparse trees and climb to a hedge/fence. Keep to its left (river) side. St Thomas's island is below in the river, with its fishing hut.

The river is tidal here at spring high water time. Cross a stile to change hedge sides and after 200m a left stile back to the left side again. Just as the path begins to turn right by the side of Horncliffemill Burn turn sharp left

Market cross at Norham

down steps (signposted) – 79 of them in total. Cross a footbridge over the burn. Follow the path as it climbs to an access track. Turn left on the track to reach the centre of Horncliffe. Turn left on the street going alongside The Fishers Arms Inn. There are 2 paths going off left. Ignore the first signed Berwick and take the second path on the left signed River Tweed. The path leads into Tofts Plantation. This is a natural wood and gives a very pleasant walk high above the Tweed. Near the end of the trees the path descends steeply to a field to regain the riverside. Union

route reverts to a path again which follows a straight course around the river bend. On the Scottish side is Paxton House, a magnificent Palladian style house built in 1758 by Patrick Home for his bride Charlotte. She was the daughter of Prussia's King Frederick the Great, but died before the wedding and never saw the house. Pass the houses of 'The Start' and

NORHAM
GR NT 900 474

Bridge can now be seen ahead and the path followed to the road at the bridge. The bridge was designed and executed by Capt S Brown in 1820 and was Britain's first suspension bridge capable of carrying road vehicles. The plaque at each end displays the motto 'Vis Unita Fortior' (Stronger in unity), symbolising the Union of England and Scotland. Chain Bridge Honey Farm is up the road to the right (open every day, free admission).

Cross the English end of the bridge and go over a stile to walk along a tarmac drive to 'The Boathouse'. Beyond the house the

'Yardford Shiel' to reach 'Low House' and a road. Walk along the road. From joining the Tweed the Scotland/England border has run along the centre of the river, deviating slightly around islands, but just before this road bends right, the border

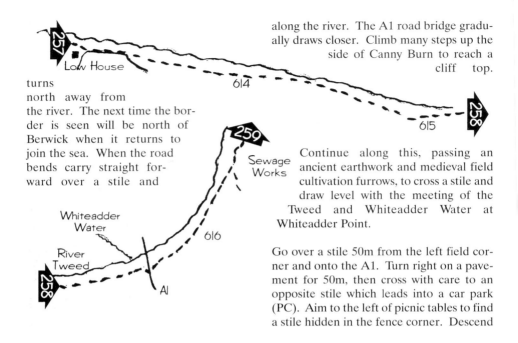

along the river. The A1 road bridge gradually draws closer. Climb many steps up the
side of Canny Burn to reach a
cliff   top.

turns
north away from
the river. The next time the border is seen will be north of
Berwick when it returns to
join the sea. When the road
bends carry straight for-
ward over a stile and

Continue along this, passing an
ancient earthwork and medieval field
cultivation furrows, to cross a stile and
draw level with the meeting of the
Tweed and Whiteadder Water at
Whiteadder Point.

Go over a stile 50m from the left field corner and onto the A1. Turn right on a pavement for 50m, then cross with care to an
opposite stile which leads into a car park
(PC). Aim to the left of picnic tables to find
a stile hidden in the fence corner. Descend

Union Bridge

Berwick ramparts

and cross a footbridge to the right (before a ruined fishing hut), then bear left to the top of the riverbank. Continue ahead with large fields to the right. Walk through 2 fields to reach a tarmac road at Toddles Shiel. Turn left for a few metres, leave the tarmac and turn left and right into a fenced passage, then right over a stile and along a fenced gravel path on the river side of the sewage works. What an end to the walk! Ah well, press on. Leave the path via a stile and continue along the sewage treatment plant fence line. Cross 250m of field (usually churned by cows) to reach a small gate. Beyond the gate walk along the high tide level. The path should be OK, but some discretion should be exercised if there is a very high tide (you could continue on the access road to the other side of the treatment works if the tide is too high).

Walk under the Royal Border Bridge and the 2 road bridges can be seen ahead. Walk on a road for 30m, then leave it on the left to rejoin the river on a tarmac path. The path soon

Royal Border Bridge

BERWICK-UPON-TWEED

617

Royal Tweed Bridge

618

Town Hall

Berwick Bridge

259

joins the road again to pass the end of the Royal Tweed Bridge. Carry on to the war memorial and turn left onto the old Berwick Bridge to cross the River Tweed. At the end of the bridge turn right below the wall, to the 3rd opening on the left with a sign 'Sally Port'. Turn left here to walk through the town wall into a small street of the same name. Turn right on Bridge Street to a junction, then turn left on Hide Hill and left again on Marygate. The Georgian Town Hall is now on the right. Walk to the end of the hall, with the old buttermarket underneath, climb 15 steps and touch one of the stone pillars of the hall. You have now completed the **GREAT ENGLISH WALK**. CONGRATULATIONS! You have achieved something most people will never do, which is to see the incredible scenery of England.

Berwick-upon-Tweed is England's most northerly town, and is one of the most outstanding fortified towns in Europe.

Nikolaus Pevsner said of the town—
One of the most exciting towns in England,
a real town, with the strongest sense of enclosure,
a town of red roofs on grey houses,
with hardly any irritating buildings anywhere
and a town of the most intricate
changes of levels.

The town's position has meant much in the relationship between England and Scotland, and it changed hands 13 times (some say 15) in the long stormy border warfare years. The English town was captured by Scotland's King Malcolm in 1018, and not recaptured until 1296 by England's Edward 1. A time of many changes then followed before the town finally became part of England in 1482.

The town fortifications were begun by Edward 1, and added to by Robert the Bruce. The walls were rebuilt however

Berwick Bridge

mainly during Elizabeth I's time. The walls are 2 miles in length and are the earliest example of gun warfare walls in Northern Europe. Berwick barracks was purpose-built by Vanburgh between 1717 and 1721, and is now open to visitors throughout the year, being operated by English Heritage.

The town has more scheduled preservation buildings than any other town of its size in England.

3 bridges cross the Tweed. Berwick Bridge dates from 1611/34 and is the 5th bridge to cross the river (others before it having collapsed). The bridge has 15 arches.

The Royal Border Bridge was designed by Robert Stephenson to carry the railway and built 1847/50. It was officially opened by Queen Victoria in 1850.

The Royal Tweed Bridge was built to relieve traffic congestion in 1925/8.

Holy Trinity Church is one of only 2 built during Cromwell's Commonwealth years. It was built in 1650/2. John Knox began his ministry from the site of the church in 1549.

The Town Hall or Guildhall is Georgian 1750/4 and has a 150 foot (46 m) spire. It used to house the Council, Police, Court and Gaol. The 8 bells are 1754, and a curfew bell is still sounded at 8.00pm.

We hope you have enjoyed the walk. Should you be just a wee bit miffed that there is a little bit of English countryside left to the north, don't despair, the Appendix covers the short distance to the border if you have the strength left.

APPENDIX
Berwick-upon-Tweed - Scottish Border
(5 miles or 8.0 km)

Berwick is the official end of the GEW, but the border is so close you may be tempted to do that little extra to reach Scotland.

Leave the Town Hall by retracing your steps and turning right into Hide Hill, then left onto Silver Street. Cross the road junction of Ravensdowne and Palace Street East and go along Ness Street to reach the Ness Gate. Pass through the town wall (the present one at this point being built between 1558 and 1570 to replace the older medieval wall), and follow the road round leftwards to pass houses and the mill of William Leith (marquee hirers). Next pass

the old Coastguard station and follow the road as it bears left to pass Pier House. Do not fork right to the beach but carry on the road as it begins to climb. When the road turns left to a car park, carry straight on along the cliff edge.

A golf course is to the left as you pass some cliff edge seats and reach the abandoned coastguard lookout point. The old *Covered Way* which led to a Redoubt is soon reached. Go left for 10m to turn right through a gap and onto the tarmac path leading to the holiday centre car park. Keep up on the cliff edge between the car-

Berwick sign

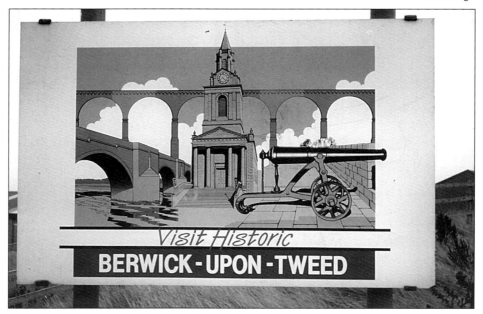

avans and the beach. Part way through the park the cliff juts out at Sharpers' Head. Eventually the end of the large caravan park is reached at a small ravine. Swing left with the path for 100m, then right (off the main path) to cross the head of the ravine and right to resume the cliff top walk.

As you walk along, with the waves tumbling onto the beach below, you can contemplate what you have achieved since you left Chepstow so long ago and so many miles away!

Snake seat, Berwick

The golf course is still to the left, but as you near the end of the fairway look down to the massively eroded cliff face below. Much further south the Cleveland Way has been breached in many parts as the land slips into the sea around the Scarborough area, but the cliffs here seem to be made of more resilient material. The beautiful Sea Plantain (Plantago maritima), with its long thin leaves, is much in evidence. The scapes (flowering stem) can be as much as 30cm in length. Thrift is also in abundance. When a fence line is reached keep to the seaward side and arrive at a fence line going inland marking the end of the golf course. A huge cultivated field is now to the left. Sea Mayweed, Lesser Burdock, Germander Speedwell, Coltsfoot and Common Knapweed are all to be found. Well over to the left the houses on the road north of Berwick come to an end. The barns of East Hope Shell oil terminal are now to your left. The mainline east coast rail-track is only 100m away. The huge field finally ends at a broken fence line and the path winds around the natural archway outcrop of Needles Eye.

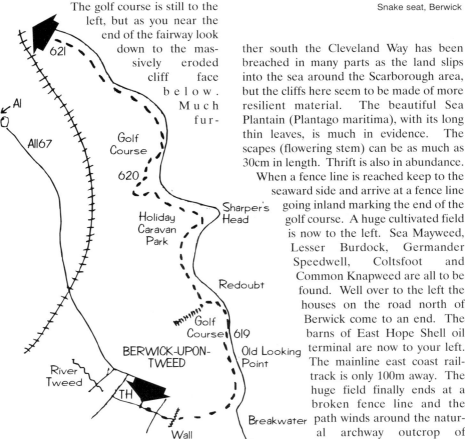

The land between the railtrack and the cliff decreases in size, bringing you close to the rail boundary, where a path takes off left over a crossing point, to cross fields to the main road. Ignore the junction and carry on along the cliff, walking between the flowers of Yarrow, Harebell and Red Campion. At St John's Haven (a small inlet) the path swings left to meet the stone rail boundary wall, before swinging right back to the cliff edge again. Marshall Meadows bay is now in view ahead. Another broken fence line is crossed into a small field (by standards in this area), and a stile over the wall to the left is reached. Cross this stile to enter another caravan park and turn right on the dirt road through the park. At the end of the park go left up

Erosion near Magdolen Fields

the incline to reach the left side of an old bridge (the path used to go under the bridge, but was re-routed and the bridge has now been filled in). Turn right to cross the bridge, and then turn half-left to strike across the field (or if under cultivation, pass round the field on the cliff edge). Having reached the far side continue to walk along to reach a double stile over a fence line. The fence marks the boundary between England and Scotland, but unfortunately has no sign to mark this fact! Over to the left, on the rail line, there is however a signpost marking the border. At last you have reached the ultimate goal.

You could carry on if you are really that keen, or return—

a. along the same path to reach Berwick or

b. to the filled in bridge and then along the road to reach the A1. There is a pavement all the way along the A1 back to Berwick.

We hope you have enjoyed your journey through the beautiful English countryside. You can now go back home for a rest!

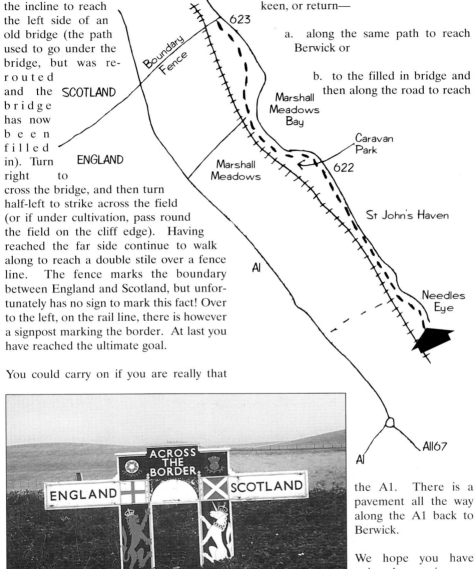

The border!

Facility List

	Inn	Accomm-odation	PO	Store	Public Conveniences
Hathersage	Y	Y	Y	Y	Y
Langsett	Y	Y	N	Y	N
Strines	Y	Y	N	N	N
Flouch	Y	Y	N	N	N
Scholes	Y	N	N	N	N
Holmfirth	Y	Y	Y	Y	Y
Upperthong	Y	N	N	N	N
Meltham	Y	Y	Y	Y	Y
Marsden	Y	Y	Y	Y	Y
Ripponden	Y	Y	Y	Y	Y
Hebden Bridge	Y	Y	Y	Y	Y
Haworth	Y	Y	Y	Y	Y
Sutton-in-Craven	Y	N	N	Y	N
Cross Hills	Y	Y	Y	Y	Y
Kildwick	Y	Y	N	N	N
Silsden	Y	N	Y	Y	N
Ilkley	Y	Y	Y	Y	Y
Pateley Bridge	Y	Y	Y	Y	Y
Kirkby Malzeard	Y	N	N	Y	N
Grewelthorpe	Y	Y	N	N	N
Masham	Y	Y	Y	Y	N
Middleham	Y	Y	Y	Y	N
Wensley	Y	N	N	N	N
Leyburn	Y	Y	Y	Y	N
Marrick	N	Y	N	N	N
Greta Bridge	Y	Y	N	N	N
Barnard Castle	Y	Y	Y	Y	Y
Eggleston	Y	Y	Y	Y	N
Stanhope	Y	Y	Y	Y	Y
Rookhope	Y	Y	Y	Y	N
Blanchland	Y	Y	Y	Y	N
Allendale	Y	Y	Y	Y	Y
Catton	Y	Y	N	N	N
Bardon Mill	Y	Y	Y	Y	N
East Twice Brewed	N	Y	N	N	N
Twice Brewed	Y	Y	N	N	N
Wark	Y	Y	Y	Y	Y
Birtley	Y	N	N	N	N

	Inn	Accomm-odation	PO	Store	Public Conveniences
Elsdon	Y	Y	N	N	Y
Whitton	N	Y	N	N	N
Rothbury	Y	Y	Y	Y	Y
Thropton	Y	Y	Y	Y	Y
Harbottle	Y	Y	N	N	N
Low Alwinton	N	Y	N	N	N
Alwinton	Y	N	N	N	N
Uswayford	N	Y	N	N	N
Wooler	Y	Y	Y	Y	Y
Ford	N	Y	Y	Y	Y
Etal	Y	N	Y	Y	Y
Norham	Y	Y	N	Y	N
Horncliffe	Y	Y	N	N	N
Berwick-upon-Tweed	Y	Y	Y	Y	Y

Alterations to text Vol two

p 56... maps refer to River Calder, this is of course the River Aire

p 53... replace 'at 2 gates...again' with 'at a stile in a fence. Turn .. '

p 54...replace '(barn to right), with '(barn converted to house to right)'

p 55... replace 'cattle grid' with 'sheep fold'

p 190..Harbottle now has PO/store (but may have subsequently closed).Blanchland& Eggleston have PC